Good Genes, Luck, Lots of Prayers

ഇരു

Bob Kascht

©2008
Nightengale Press
A Nightengale Media LLC Company

GOOD GENES, LUCK, LOTS OF PRAYERS

Copyright ©2008 by Bob Kascht
Cover Design ©2008 by Nightengale Press

For information about Nightengale Press please
visit our website at www.nightengalepress.com.
Email: publisher@nightengalepress.biz
or send a letter to:
Nightengale Press
10936 N. Port Washington Road. Suite 206
Mequon, WI 53092

Library of Congress Cataloging-in-Publication Data

Kascht, Bob,
GOOD GENES, LUCK, LOTS OF PRAYERS/ Bob Kascht
ISBN:1-933449-64-0
ISBN 13: 978-1933449-64-7
Memoir

Copyright Registered: 2008
First Published by Nightengale Press in the USA

September 2008

10 9 8 7 6 5 4 3 2 1

Printed in the USA and the UK

TO MARY

Love is like a red, red rose,
Or so it has been stated,
But red is too sure,
So very secure,
It may have been overrated.

Yellow is the touch of early morn
That invites the birds to sing,
And unveils the promise
Of the opening day
With all its wondrous things.

Red is not the one I chose,
For me a gentle yellow rose,

My Mary.

Gratitude X Four

Without Mary I wouldn't have lasted this long, I wouldn't have known love, and I wouldn't have written this.

Without Jackie, there wouldn't be a Book. She transformed a Skillet-scramble into a soufflé.

Valerie very skillfully midwifed it.

John helped make it look like the real thing, and provided Zen massages at crucial times when I was too Germanic.

...and Hannibal crossed the Alps.

Chapter 1

A Mission Statement from the CEO

I have dallied for some time with these reflections on my life, rolling them from one side of my brain to the other, like savoring a delicacy, reluctant to swallow it. Only lately have I accepted the discipline of actually writing this, and now that I am, it seems presumptuous, as if writing about my life really made any difference. It feels uncomfortably egocentric, but I find reassurance in the excuse Thoreau offered, that he used *I* so often because there was no one else he knew as well.

After I had written a number of these reflections, a well intentioned friend, who was a confidant and an unofficial critic, suggested I read something by Russell Baker that would be an example of how to do it, and provide inspiration. Unfortunately, it didn't have that happy effect. I was intimidated. I cannot speak about the titans who direct the world. Nor have I interviewed presidents, or ranged over continents reporting the great movements of mankind or the cataclysms that disrupt society. I can only write of the little things and the common people who were part of my life. This is a melange, within the purview of ordinary people, that might evoke similar memories.

My life contained some elements of classic drama, but in the actual living it was quite mundane. It was sufficiently troubled and complicated to qualify, but the cast was disappointing, composed of simple, sincere people, without much daring or imagination, who were drudging toward predictable outcomes. Perhaps I just didn't know how to exploit the possibilities. Very possibly, life around the great ones wasn't so high-pitched until Fate applied a touch of flavor enhancer.

These memories were registered in detail, on a fine grain emulsion, and with full flavor. Thankfully, the retrieval is printed in gentle sepia, softening some of the glare and pain. I am now in a quiet time, a holding pattern, awaiting the landing. I am writing for grandchildren and for those yet unborn, for a time in the future when I will not be here. I hope our children can gain increased appreciation of our earnest efforts, and our love for them. As a side benefit, I should like those who follow to realize that we were more than just faded photographs, alive and "full of beans". It would be the ideal reward if they wish they had known us.

Chapter 2

And It Came to Pass

In the great world of global affairs, June 10, 1921, wasn't a momentous occasion, but in the microcosm of the Kascht and Rubert families it rivaled the *Big Bang* that allegedly sparked the universe. A star shone over eastern Iowa, and Bob was born.

This was otherwise a calm interval between crises and disasters. "The War to End All Wars" had turned the world inside out, and was passing into the mellow stage of historical perspective. Without awareness of it, people were rushing toward a great depression, and in their ignorance they reveled in the material good life. It was a carnival of flappers, the Charleston, short skirts and wild hats, prohibition, speakeasies, violence and convenient morals. Money was something to be made without thought or effort, and spent with zest and flourish. Corrupt politicians and grand scandals spawned a disillusioned and turbulent working class.

Bob was suited to these time, the drab and the sparkling, the good and the bad, all the opposites, and both sides of the coin, having been born in the sign of Gemini, with two fluctuant and unstable natures.

He had been a long and painful labor, a fact which his mother repeated in frequent petulant moments. Not to slip into the world unnoticed, as just another birth, Bob dramatized the situation by obstinately refusing to wet his diapers. After twenty four hours the tension built, and this assumed a menacing portent. Godparents were hastily assembled, and he was Baptized. Perhaps it was the pouring of the water, or perhaps there had just been a satisfying amount of commotion, so Bob relented and the crisis was resolved. This was the favored interpretation of some elders who had observed the Kascht mindset in various manifestations.

Chapter 3

Just the Facts

After all the commotion on my arrival, things settled down and became so routine as to be almost inert. For the sake of completeness, and to provide perspective, I have summarized my early life with a sweeping broad brush, for a wide angle view. This risks presenting too much generality, and not leaving enough room for detail. It covers a lot of time and distance, but hopefully not at the cost of color and vitality. I avoided the Genesis genealogic style of cataloging who begat whom, because I did not want this to have the charm of a telephone directory.

I was born in Waterloo, Iowa. My father had just begun his dental practice there. After two or three years he moved to a nearby community, Jesup, population about six hundred. I have no idea what thought went into this decision, but I vaguely recall hearing him say that he would rather be a large frog in a small puddle than the reverse. This sounds so trite. I doubt that it really meant much to him, and it certainly didn't explain anything to me at the age of four.

About this time I was joined by a brother. Probably I didn't welcome him. I don't remember much about it, but mother had informed me a number of times that I once stood over him as he lay on the floor, with a large pair of shears aimed down at him, as if I intended to drop them point first. I don't believe I would have been so openly hostile. Moreover, it isn't my nature to be so obvious.

I began first grade in the Jesup school at the age of five without the benefit of kindergarten. I could read quite well then, and was taken to other classes to show off. My most vivid memory of first or second grade concerns a little boy who tried to bully me. I don't recall the circumstances, but the boy's name was Lyle Brown, and he was the son of the blacksmith. For whatever reason, I hit him in the nose, and he ran home dripping blood. I was greatly surprised and thought I would be in big trouble, so I followed him home and kicked snow to cover the blood spots. My father probably was surprised, but I don't remember any consequences.

When I was about eight years old, my father discovered he had TB. It was necessary for him to discontinue dentistry. We moved to grandpa's farm to live in a tent for the healing benefits of fresh air. Then we moved back to Waterloo, and mother got a job, or rather a succession of jobs. We moved four times, and I attended four different schools. My father said, in an attempt at feeble humor, that it was cheaper to move than to pay rent. Incidentally, rent in those days for our type of house was twenty two dollars a month.

I was a good Catholic, surviving the nuns at Sacred Heart, St. Mary's, and St John's. After eighth grade it was necessary to switch to the public schools, because we could not afford the tuition of a Catholic high school. I don't have any awareness that I suffered much damage from this forced change. I did well at East High, and was into everything from the newspaper to student council and theater. I was also a cheer leader, which always surprised me, because I considered myself as quiet and somewhat withdrawn. I was, in my view, socially inferior because of the limitations of our family, and our lack of money.

I was a good student, and graduated. There was not much talk about scholarships in those days. My father had died when I was a sophomore, and it was assumed I would just go to work. Somehow,

I quietly hatched the idea that I would attend Iowa State Teacher's College in Cedar Falls, ten miles away. I did this, and worked second shift at the Rath Meat Packing Company for four years. Then I enlisted in the army after Pearl Harbor was attacked. The army sent me to medical school at Northwestern University in Chicago. After that I interned in Milwaukee, taught at Marquette, did some residency time in Internal Medicine in a New York City hospital, and then returned to Milwaukee for a residency in Pathology. I married, and quite soon after was coerced into accepting a commission in the Air Force.

Reliving many of these memories is painful. Some of it may be dull to the outsider, but in real time it was a bushel of misery. This happened before ***Angela's Ashes,*** and I didn't have any awareness that suffering was salable, but my not being Irish would have been a limitation. I have written about a few of the more dramatic or problematic side trips that made my life story occasionally more like a travelogue than just a plain road map.

Chapter 4

Frank Rubert

Grandpa Frank was the best butcher in Perry township, and probably in all of Buchanan county. I know it was so, because he told me himself. Before he moved to the farm, he had owned a meat market in Waterloo, a nearby city of about forty thousand. He had considered each of these a potential customer who needed to discover his services. Such was his confidence. He was a handsome man, very much a dandy. Hanging behind the meat counter was a large framed picture of him seated on his delivery wagon, with a team of sleek black horses hitched in oiled, shiny harnesses. The side panel of the wagon had a sign: *Quality Meats—F.C. Rubert.*

He had printed postcards of this made, and a stack of them lay on the top of the display case, ready to be mailed. His satisfied customers were invited to share the good news with friends everywhere, even if they weren't within his service range. This was uncommonly enterprising for those times, but totally consistent with the character of the man perched on the delivery wagon, wearing a derby, a striped green and white shirt and a bow tie. It probably did little to attract customers, but it was positive assurance to those who came in that they were in the best place possible. In the picture he was serious, almost stern, full of the confidence and resolve you would expect from the man who was providing your meat. He had deliberately chosen this demeanor as more appropriate for the purpose than his usual smile. He was especially proud of his teeth. All of the original ones were present without a single cavity when he died at the age of sixty six.

He was an enjoyable outgoing man, and although I never really knew what it meant, in the terms of those days he was a *kidder.* His background education was never discussed, undoubtedly the usual one room school variety, but it had yielded good results. He read easily and wrote with a Spencerian flourish, that all my parochial school Palmer method couldn't equal. His signature on checks was a distinctive evidence of confidence and self-satisfaction. He spoke flowingly and with obvious enjoyment. He had a ready supply of stories, most of which I didn't understand, or didn't get to hear. I sensed they were marginal, because grandma hovered nearby and gave her pious *tsk, tsk* trying to protect me, or at least neutralize the effect.

From the earliest days, I remember looking at his hands. They were neat and clean, but not unusual. I expected something remarkable, because he had often repeated that people frequently asked if he was weighing his thumb again. I certainly expected to see a giant digit, but this was just his concession to butcher humor. I don't know how he came to be a butcher. No one ever talked about it, and it probably didn't occur to him to say. In those days there were limited career options, and he probably just stumbled into it without any directed burning ambition, but he was good at it.

Doubtless, he could have succeeded at many other things. In another time he might have been a politician or an advertising whiz, but as a butcher he was so successful that he expanded his horizon and opened a restaurant. Grandma was an excellent cook, and she had the ideal Irish personality for serving the public, so he installed her next door in a venture that was pretentiously named *The Grand Cafe.* She learned quickly, grew in confidence and became a clever manager and business woman. She acquired dignity and grace and was accepted into the social order of the community. With three young daughters blooming into nubile debutantes to provide atmosphere, and occasional help, the Grand Cafe became a popular spot on the Waterloo map. From many stories and recollections, faded photographs, yellowed newspaper ads and souvenir menus, it is evident that they were very successful in their joint enterprise. The family had all the amenities and material comforts, and the daughters were displayed in their finery with the same assurance as the family of a New York tycoon. They enjoyed their lives fully.

₨₧

My mother was the youngest of the three daughters, and in that favored position, she was indulged and undoubtedly spoiled. She was always Kitten to her father. Pictures show her as beautiful and quite high fashion. It appears that the family lived very comfortably, from abundant furs to a Kissel touring car. Despite this affluence, my mother considered the name Rubert to be disappointing. She thought she had read that the owner of the New York Yankees, Colonel Jacob Rupert, was of French descent. She concluded that the "B" in Rubert must have been a clerical error, committed by an indifferent low level clerk in the bureau of vital statistics someplace, and that her name really should be spelled with a "P," which was so much more elegant. As she said so often throughout her life, "It is a known fact." Unfortunately, she wasn't able to convince her usually subservient father, who seemed annoyingly content with his good life, his good looks and his peasant station.

Mother pursued this, pumping the memories of the aunts, rummaging through stacks of yellowed letters, and challenging the spelling in the most official of all records, in three family Bibles. None of these sources supported her quest. Grandpa Frank's father had a first name of doubtful origin, Bezelar or Belezar, which caused her to shudder. It suggested an itinerant Armenian rug peddler, rather than a refined, princely Frenchman. Sadly, he was long departed, and could add nothing to upgrading mother's social image. She survived this tragic letdown, and in the abundant energy and bloom of her late teens, she dedicated herself to the Charleston and the Black Bottom. At some point she concluded that she would marry my father who was an unsuspecting medical student at far away Creighton University.

There was a slight impediment. He was a Catholic, she was Presbyterian. Undoubtedly, there were exciting negotiating skirmishes, but in the interest of true love and family harmony she converted to Catholicism. As she described it, this wasn't a profound theologic event. She had a few *instructions* from the local priest, and she was in. Grandpa and grandma were wonderfully peaceful and supportive, but they didn't pretend to understand what the Roman church was all about, or what all that fancy Latin had to do with anything. This was a shining tribute to their pragmatic character.

ೞೞ

It is impossible to reconstruct a feasible scenario for what came next. With the daughters launched on their individual paths, Frank and Carrie decided to move to the farm. It is presumptuous, from a perspective decades later, to ascribe motives, or even to pretend to understand it. They were established and very successful in their joint ventures.

What had happened? What could explain why the grandparents would leave a seemingly ideal life. Perhaps, the fact that they were both born on farms, and were deeply imprinted with an instinct for the simple way of life. Whatever the truth, they sold their holdings in the city, bought a farm of one hundred twenty acres, and moved.

The nearest community, an unmapped crossroad cluster of houses, was fittingly named Littleton. This was near their birthplaces, and where they had begun their married life. That may be the simple answer, emotion over logic.

There were no buildings on the farm. It presented only the potential of world class Iowa loam. In the final days, during the closing of their lives in Waterloo, they built a chicken house, reasoning that this would be storage and the operational base for the building of their house. What happened next seemed so unlikely it suggested a whimsical, or even vindictive, fate. The site had been selected, high ground near the road, about a hundred yards from the area designated for the animal pens and a like distance from the hickory woods on the other side. Excavation of the basement began. As the bottom was reached, the hole started to fill with water. A spring had been uncovered. Springs were not common in that part of the country, and if located at a different place on the farm, this one would have been most welcome as a source of water for the animals. An unsuccessful attempt was made to cap the spring. It was abandoned.

What to do? The family had indeed crossed its Rubicon; there was no turning back. It was suggested that a dowser might apply his mysterious talent in reverse, finding a place where there wasn't water. The options were limited. With the war driving the economy, prices of building materials soared unrealistically, and the original budget was abandoned. Reluctantly, the grandparents were forced to accept the idea of adapting the chicken house for their use as a home, at least temporarily. Grandma was the one who felt the greatest disruption in this revised plan. The farm was still the same. The soil was as black and fertile as ever. The fields could be planted, and the animals could be pastured, and housed in a makeshift straw roofed pole barn. Grandma's burden was to impart magic to the henhouse, and transform it into a home, and that she did.

GOOD GENES, LUCK, LOTS OF PRAYERS

On a small knoll, rising green out of the dark of the fields, the few buildings clustered as if for mutual support, a barn, a corncrib, and a chicken house. In the middle of what was the front yard, a ragged hollow testified that once upon a time a basement had been dug and abandoned. Weeds partially repaired this, with meandering unconcern. The family settled into the chicken house. Sheets of cardboard separated the bedrooms from the kitchen and all-purpose living room. The floor was covered, but not softened or warmed, by cheap linoleum. The walls were brightened with flowery paper, and the little chicken house became as quaintly livable as any regular abode on the surrounding prairie.

Much has been written about the farm, mostly by poets or artists or naturalists. Few of them had ever lived on a farm, so they idealized and fantasized with abandon about the freedom and unending inspiration. For some it was a hobby; for others it was an ecology experiment, but it was mostly academic and theoretic. The actual life on the farm was hard and demanding. The intimate relationship with the earth and the forces of nature did produce deference to a higher power, and growing things gave a subtle sense of sharing in creation, but day after dreary day sameness could lead to depression and even suicide. The land took little notice, and rolled on endlessly, deceptively docile. It presented a challenge, but allowed men the illusion they were in control. They planned, and plowed and planted, and all the while, the earth and its partner, the weather, conserved their awesome forces for the times when they would capriciously remind those transient intruders, who the real masters of nature were. Yet, in this ongoing struggle, the settlers rebounded time after time from fire, draught, flood, tornado or blizzard, and rooted themselves ever deeper in the soil. There was no time to develop the arts, or appreciate the wonders of this so-called good life. Very few farmers had ever heard of Thoreau. There was one distinctive derivative of this way of life. Men on the farm did not leave daily to go to a factory or store. Meager as their lives were, they worked where they lived, on their own land. This agrarian form of unity produced an intense sense of independence and freedom. It was the essence of the founding fathers, but despite this high-sounding principle, farmers were grubbingly indentured to their crops and their animals. This commitment to the everyday care of the livestock was collectively called *chores*. It was the metronome that pulsed the cadence of the lives of the farm folk, men and women. It was inexorable. As one farm poet wrote: "The image of God clad in overalls, daily enters the barn, and there fails his divinity, because cows bawl on Sunday." Was this a life one would choose if given an option?

I had always been in the favored position of visiting the farm, living there all summer and being too young to have burdensome duties. It was a fantasy mix of dreams and nursery rhymes. The world was anything I wanted it to be. I might gather eggs, pull a few weeds or carry in an armload of kindling for the cookstove. In retrospect this was something like being a grandparent who could play all day with the children, then go home at night and leave the problems to the parents. On my ninth birthday, I had a try at being grown-up, but it failed, and I lapsed back to being eight for a couple of years. Inevitably, this fantasy stage passed, and I was initiated into the work world.

Milking was especially boring. Even the cows seemed to feel that way, as they stared blankly into space, chewed their everpresent cud and indifferently tolerated the intrusion. We tried to liven this by giving them names of movie stars. We had Clara Bow, Myrna Loy, Pola Negri and for obvious reasons, Mae West. We did target practice on the cat. Nothing made any difference. It still had to be done morning and evening.

Feeding pigs was slightly more exciting than watching grass grow. They had no individuality. From birth they were just one of a line-up on either side of the mother's ample cafeteria, hanging on to survive. Later, I poured pailfulls of milk and healthful ingredients into a trough that was full of pigs' front feet. There was rumbling and grunting and squealing. The next day the same thing, and the next and the next. Because it was so unvarying, there didn't appear to be any change. Then, one day grandpa would say, "Well, I guess they're ready." The next day the feet in the trough were little and pink, and it started all over again.

There were some compensations. I worked my way up to helping with threshing. This was the most exciting event of the year, the high point of the seasonal cycle. It was probably the most successful development in the evolution of American farming. It was an arrangement for getting the work done, and it also provided an occasion for social contact that was infrequent. In this system ten or twelve neighboring farmers agreed to help each other harvest and thresh the grain, usually oats. They contracted with someone who had a threshing machine and a steam engine to pull it and provide the power drive. At the proper time the man and his machine appeared. The afternoon before it was our turn, I sat at the front gate waiting for the first sight and sound. I could hear the steamer and see the belching smoke as soon as it left the neighboring farm. When it arrived, looking like an ungainly animal with a long neck being hauled by a noisy jerky black engine, grandpa, as the host farmer, had the authority to indicate how and where he wanted it set up. This was done, the wheels were blocked, the drive belt attached and the engine was turned off for the night. I couldn't sleep; this was bigger than the circus. The next morning after chores, the neighbors with teams of horses and haywagons began to arrive, and started hauling in the shocks of oats. The steamer and threshing machine started up and threshing was underway. Now I was fourteen, and was allowed, or expected, to run the oat wagon. This involved directing the spout from the machine to deliver the oats evenly until the wagon was filled, and then call for another wagon. This was the main purpose of the entire project. I was surprised that I had been given this much responsibility. Best of all, I was really working and would be allowed to eat dinner with the men. This was the high point of the day. In past years I had to eat after the men, with the girls who cleaned the dishes.

Threshing was a festival for the entire family. For the men it was sharing the work and connecting in friendship, something that was often lacking in this lonely, independent way of life. For the hostess it was a day in the center stage spotlight. Throughout the year the ladies had frequent opportunities at church socials to showcase their talents. The highest cakes, the best boiled frosting, the latest secret seasoning in the salad, blended with the most shocking truths about someone who wasn't there, unofficially established a hierarchy. Everyone knew who was the best cook, even though it would never be openly agreed on. However, at threshing time, each woman in her turn, was queen for the day. She orchestrated and commanded. In simple fact, the options were very limited. The menu was prescribed. There must be three kinds of meat, beef, pork and chicken. Mashed potatoes were the only acceptable accompaniment. Three kinds of vegetables allowed for slight variation, but no foolishness like parsnips or squash. Dessert was cake and pie, probably two varieties of each. After all the main meal, every man was still expected to sample both, and recognize the wonderful flaky crust made with the finest leaf lard. With the playing field so level and the rules so rigidly limiting, how could any woman hope to excel her neighbor, and yet each quietly felt she had. Only the men really knew, and they reported the truth at home that night, where reputations were made or destroyed.

The young neighbor girls also had their inning. They were brought by their mothers to round out the work force and spare older legs. There was also a subliminal motivation, to parade the budding nubile generation of females before an audience of vulnerable young males. Many traced their earliest surges of *awareness* to the day they first saw their future wife bouncing, appealingly flushed and moist, between the trestle tables, innocently bumping an arm or tripping and brushing against a back or shoulder.

After this exhausting twenty minute frenzy, it was time for the traditional *farmer's nap.* Everyone laid down in the yard, hats covering the face, and hands folded over rounded bellies. The older, experienced men could be asleep in less than a minute. It was a mark of rank and success if one could snore. It was a scene of serenity from the Elysian fields. Ten minutes was the limit, and then back to work, presumably refreshed, but it often took an hour to recover from the refueling overload. By mid-afternoon I began to worry that I would do the unthinkable and falter, maybe even ask for someone to help, but this wasn't acceptable. For most of the farms of our size, threshing was completed in one day. The machinery was then prepared to travel to the next farm. The farmers said good-by, see you tomorrow, and thank the wife. There was one slight variation from this. The farmer for tomorrow's session added to the routine: "Frank, I been watching your boy working the oats wagon. If you could spare him tomorrow, I'd like it if you brought him along."

In the Midwest we didn't spend much time talking fancy about rites of passage. It is supposed to have something to do with growing up. I had read about it. There is a great variety, from someone wearing a grotesque mask or painted up and doing a sweaty dance, to an intellectualized ceremony like a Bar Mitzvah. This recognizes that the young candidate is now ready to perform an essential function in the tribe or community, and it exhibits his acceptance of this new responsibility. In my life, getting to start the model A and run the oats wagon took care of all that. Things just don't get any better.

೮೧೧೪

With few exceptions, things went smoothly through the years. I often went to the farm on weekends. It was very much a second home, and the grandparents provided much needed stability during the time when my father was ill. They were conscientious about taking me to an Irish neighbor so I could get to mass on Sunday. At times I preferred to go with them to their little country church, and I became very familiar with *"Jesus Wants Me for a Sunbeam"* and other understandable hymns. No religious sensitivity ever surfaced in the family, but on one occasion grandpa felt a touch of the bigotry that lurked among the neighbors. One morning he went to bring in the horses from the pasture and discovered that someone had painted three large black "K"s on a white horse. The general implication was obvious, someone was watching and wanted to send a message. Grandpa was not a man to be intimidated, and nothing more happened. Unfortunately, when Grandpa decided to move to the farm it was a mistake. He was not a successful farmer. Fundamentally, he was a people person and most of this indefinable quality was lost on the animals or the solitude of the fields. Moreover, he was too fastidious. He picked up little bits of trash that blew around the farm; he refused to plant a tree near the house, because it would drop leaves on the lawn. He often wore gloves. This was viewed with some question and may have been considered an affectation by his neighbors. His cleanliness, which served so well in the meat market, set him uncomfortably, slightly apart from the average farmer. His apron, which had been an expanse of white, was a contrast to his competitors, who customarily wiped bloody hands on their fronts, and looked as if something disastrous had happened in the back room.

GOOD GENES, LUCK, LOTS OF PRAYERS

৩০৫৪

The nearest we came to any religious conflict was over the issue of eating meat on Friday. This provided an enjoyable opportunity for me to triumph. Regularly, on Friday, Grandpa made a trip to Waterloo to deliver chickens that he, and a makeshift crew of neighbor women, had picked and processed the afternoon before. I usually rode home with him after school for a weekend visit. Routinely, Grandpa would buy a prime cut of meat, selected and saved for him by one of his cronies from the olden times, when he delivered to their shops. This brought into focus one of the major practical differences in our religions. It wasn't high level theology, but in the black or white pre-Vatican II days, Catholicism was either golden pageantry and incense or gray original sin. For the crime of Adam, we were required to suffer and deny ourselves worldly pleasures. That was translated to mean, "No meat on Friday." Grandpa, being a mere Presbyterian, was spared this denial. He could eat meat on Friday, and this he usually did, especially if I was visiting. With teasing graciousness he would pass the platter of meat to me, and I would piously decline, thus fulfilling my self-image of modern day martyrdom. The scenario called for him to say solicitously, "Oh, I'm sorry Bobby, I forgot, it's Friday." The accompanying twinkle betrayed the depth of his apology. To compound this sacrifice, I had to eat fried eggs, or for a very sinful week, fish. Those were the days before Birdseye had invented flash freezing and took the penance out of Friday. We had real fish that had spent a lifetime roiling the muddy bottom of the local river, and gave off a cooking odor that discouraged the appetite in advance. The alternative included canned salmon, with its gray skin and stacked vertebrae that had been so softened by the canning process that grandma didn't bother to remove them. You just thought that the crunchy stuff was onions or celery.

However, Mother Church moves in mysterious ways. When a Holyday happened to fall on Friday, the rules changed, and school was out, quite literally. It was the special way of honoring the memory of the holy ones. Rules were suspended, and we could even eat meat. Naturally, most of us did, so as not to squander the opportunity or to seem ungrateful to the saint who had arranged it. It happened just like that one particular Friday. I was at the farm and grandpa made his usual gracious gesture of offering the steak platter to me. "Would you like a piece, Bobby?" I accepted eagerly, and slid two large pieces onto my plate. Grandpa was flustered. He fumbled and stuttered and finally got out the question, "Don't you remember, it's Friday?" I smiled innocently and kept on chewing without apparent ill effect, or even remorse. He couldn't comprehend the basic level theologic explanation I offered. All he knew was that an Absolute, a categorical imperative, had been violated. Of course he didn't know it in those words, just the fact that something very fundamental in the world had changed. He had been betrayed, and he was still hungry. He tried a feeble move, "I'll share it with you, Bobby," but I had a mouth full and didn't answer. This was the ultimate treachery and deceit. From that day on, Grandpa viewed me with the same hesitant suspicion he had for the Pope.

ΒΙℭƦ

A Touch of Pride

I have never seen a toothbrush displayed among the funerary artifacts of a pharaoh or in the burial mounds of the pre-Columbian Indians. It is an unlikely thing to represent the whole of a man's being, but it capsulizes a significant facet of my grandpa Frank.

After every meal he brushed his teeth. For this purpose he used plain water, and loudly swished it around in his mouth. In the morning he chose to start the day with a flavor and preferred to use tooth powder. Doctor Lyon's was in vogue then. This was before tooth paste had been popularized. Occasionally he would add salt or baking soda. It seemed like a random impulse, but he viewed it as a solemn and deliberate formulation. Eventually Ipana appeared on the commercial horizon, and since we listened every week to the Ipana radio hour, he felt morally obligated to use it. Whatever the truth may turn out to be regarding the efficacy of the various dentifrices, grandpa was a shining proof that something really worked. All that was needed was a university study to determine what.

Grandpa showed his teeth readily. Much of the time he was smiling, and it presented a chicken-or-egg dilemma, which was first, the teeth that demanded to be displayed, or the smile which required that he make his teeth worthy of the opportunity. The former seemed more likely, because even when he wasn't smiling, he had a way of relaxing his lips and slightly opening his mouth that allowed a small glint. These were not the brilliant porcelain white favored by the early cinemas. Rather, they were light yellow, true ivory, not artificial but organic, genuine and functional.

All of his concerns and care were rewarded. At the time of his death in his late sixties, all of his teeth were present and intact, without a single filling. He had been ideally equipped to be the earthy, meaty robust man he was. As I approached the coffin at his wake, I almost expected to see that he had been prepared with a wide smile, to make a final display.

Chapter 5

Grandma Rubert

Carrie Smith was born in the early 1870's, in northeastern Iowa. This was an awesome expanse of open prairie, rarely fenced or broken by a plow, beautiful, but often harsh. The rules were simple and direct. It was survival, something between frontier violence and an organized social order. The extremes of the frontier had moved to the West, where gold and Sitting Bull were competing forces. In Iowa, only straggling families of Indians still rode their shaggy ponies across the horizon, stopping at times, asking for food, and frightening the children and women. For the settlers there was no sense of destiny, no drama or romance, just monotonous variations of gray.

In this void, little Carrie learned, during sixteen hour days, the chores and skills essential for a country woman. She gained the strength and stoic resignation that enabled the pioneers to endure. She trudged to the white one room school house that had been mandated by congress. Bright and quick, she learned what the limited teachers could offer, and then herself passed the exam to qualify as a teacher. She never taught, but she had a distinguishing certificate that assured her she could. In the course of maturing, she married a neighboring young man, Frank Rubert, in 1893. He had been raised in a similar farm setting by his grandparents, but by some impulse, he had become a butcher. They lived in a small crossroad community on the banks of the Wapsipinnicon river. It was an idyllic setting. Three daughters were borne to them in the next six years. They were given musical names that promised serenity and virtue, Eunice, Delight and Esther. Inevitably, the family outgrew the limited opportunities of that world, and they moved to the city in 1910.

Waterloo was flush with pre-war prosperity, not knowing the sacrifices and disaster ahead. Grandpa started his meat market, and soon grandma was installed in a restaurant next door. The daughters found an exciting new universe, and set out to conquer it. The two older ones were restless and adventuresome, and after high school each left. Eunice tested the big city, wherever that was, and Delight, certain her piano and voice would open vaudeville to her, ended in Birmingham, and was heard from only sporadically. Esther stayed home. By the time the Armistice was signed, Grandma and Grandpa were ready for the next stage of their lives.

Under ordinary circumstances, returning to the farm would have been traumatic for grandma. She had left the small community to go to the city as a tenuous country girl. Now she was a mature, confident and accomplished woman. Her world had contracted, but she refused to let it pinch or constrict her. She had lived the good life with all its amenities, and developed a strong need for people and a social life. She was forceful and buoyant. She would not become isolated, so she became a presence in the small community, and entertained everyone who came to the farm, from the Watkins spice salesman to the itinerant student ministers who drove ninety miles each Sunday to get a sense of pastoral duties in the real world.

Grandma was a paradox within herself, a farm girl with a twinkling Irish spirit, restrained in the type-cast mold of a Presbyterian matron. She was a sturdy woman, and at five feet two and about one hundred sixty pounds, something of a dumpling, certainly not statuesque or imposing. She aged gracefully, without artifice. Her skin was smooth, unaided by cosmetics. Even in later years she had few wrinkles, although she acquired a slight wattle. Her face was forever soft; she never beetled or frowned. Her hair was curly, requiring only a dash of water and the flip of a comb to break into ringlets. In her nineties she was only slightly streaked with gray. The palest of blue eyes dominated her face. You could almost look through them to the inside, but in the rare moments when she was angry they darkened and snapped at you. She looked at people with individual focused attention, not darting around searching for someone more important. She would have been an ideal Dale Carnegie model. When she looked at me, there was a special light, and I knew she loved me.

Dark clouds appeared on the horizon, and stormed her life with tragedy. Eunice, the oldest daughter, had married and was abandoned by a temporary husband. She returned home, delivered a son, and then sickened and died. Delight, the second daughter, came home from wherever she was, without much explanation, and also died. Both were buried in the prime Iowa soil of the family plot in the Littleton cemetery. For farm people, dying was a familiar event, affecting animals and humans, and even the cycle of sowing and reaping highlighted it as a stage in the continuum of life. It was accepted as a sooner or later fact. There was sorrow and awareness of loss, but the cows still had to be milked twice a day. Now Carrie faced her most daunting challenge, making a home in the henhouse, but she knew she could do it.

It wasn't a newlywed's dream cottage. Chicken houses developed to serve a function, and they were very much one size fits all, with little individuality. The design was long and narrow to keep the chickens spread out, reducing crowding or smothering, and abundant windows to assure cross ventilation. The one that was destined to be called home, was forty feet long and twenty feet wide. It was a standard model with a high sloping back roof , and just below the peak, on the front, was a row of clerestory windows. From this a shorter front roof extended. Beneath this, at ground level, was a similar full length row of windows. Just beneath the soffit on the back wall was a full length drop board, hinged to open, providing cross ventilation. The most intimidating feature of all was the concrete floor. Throughout the years, it was the only feature about which grandma complained. It was hard and cold, and there was no way to modify it. The standard interior decorating wisdom was worthless. That had evolved for traditional rooms with dividing walls. Slick magazines selling paint and paper and promoting furniture arrangements provided little inspiration. Grandma solved the problem, always with the expectation it was only temporary, by hanging bed sheets to separate two bed rooms. Admittedly, this lacked privacy. Very little of their furniture was suitable. It was out of place, or it had no essential function in this Spartan setting. The floor was covered with linoleum which did nothing to change the basic quality of cement. There were only outside walls, so hanging things was limited. Free standing chests and a chiffonier were jammed in between the beds. A piano usurped living space, but was considered a good trade off, and became the focal point of many warm gatherings. Grandma had a four hole cook stove, with an oven and a reservoir to hold water for heating. Next to it was a large barrel shaped chunk burner that had to provide the heat for the entire living space. It was inadequate for the periphery, but close up it could roast meat. It was a serious responsibility to keep this going continuously during winter nights. The rest of the furnishings were eclectic, making their way into permanent status because they served a purpose. Most of this could be classed as Country Primitive and Mission Oak in the fads of later generations. A few treasured remembrances of the old life were carefully packed away, never used and rarely viewed. The traditional wedding gift of Haviland, twelve place settings, was newspaper wrapped, stuffed in a laundry boiler and stored in the barn, waiting for an occasion that would justify using it.

Grandma bustled through the succession of sixteen hour days, endlessly repeating themselves. Providing three meals every day was the primary duty. The men were launched into the morning field work with a breakfast of scrambled eggs, potatoes, steak saved from supper and pie. She baked cookies and cakes, made rhubarb or apple sauce, worked in the garden, picked and prepared and canned vegetables. She fed the chickens and collected eggs, and sold some for her secret petty cash purse. She continually organized and revised the menu for three approximately equal meals each day. It was widely acknowledged that she cooked the best chicken, canned the prettiest tomatoes and grew the crispiest radishes. There also was laundry, darning socks, patching overalls, polishing the stoves to the deepest black and waxing the linoleum. Most impressive was her quiet acceptance that this was the way life was, and should be. There was no grumbling to suggest that she might feel a bit overwhelmed. She had one habit that stands out in memory. As she worked, she whistled under her breath, never breaking into a tune, but from the tempo and phrasing, one could tell what it was. Most often it was a hymn. In this almost subliminal manner, I was introduced to *"Bringing in the Sheaves"* or *"The Old Rugged Cross"* and many other standards of the faith. When I accompanied her to services, I was amazed that these tuneless renderings had effectively conveyed the essential flavor, and thus prepared, I sang along with the congregation.

Pleasant View Church celebrated its centennial when I was about eight. It had an enrollment of slightly over eighty parishioners, and assuming a one to one ratio, I assume there were also eighty souls, as the minister always referred to them. There was little theology. *Church* meant getting dressed up on Sunday, maybe even in a new pair of overalls, and going to sing mightily, and fidget through the Bible readings and the performance of student preachers who came to practice so they might get into the big time. For grandma, the frequent potluck suppers in the church basement were the principal attraction. The auxiliary ladies exhibited their best recipes, and competed in a self-effacing, but quietly ferocious manner. It was carefully noted, whose dish was emptied first. The best cook was never officially decided and crowned, but there was grudging deference, and within themselves, the ladies conceded the peck order. Grandma had substantial support for this honor. The standard uniform of the day was a print dress and a hat squarely fixed with a long black pin, but this was also an opportunity to showcase any new clothing or adornment. Unvaryingly the ladies were powdered white and lily of the valley sweet, starched and girdled by fashion's decree and by their religious beliefs.

Grandma kept her two worlds in balance. She relied on the church to assure that she was on the road to salvation, and that she also was fully appreciated by her neighbors. Beyond her home duties and the diversions of the church society, she looked across the fields and knew the wonder of natural beauty and freedom, things that many of the neighbors missed. She was content.

Chapter 6

Max

My cousin, Max, was shot in the eye with a BB gun when he was nine years old, and it ruined his life. He was six years older than me. My mother and his were sisters. From little things I heard as a boy, she was the adventuresome one in the family. She played the piano and sang, and thought she could be an entertainer. She left the farm, "Ran away," they said, with a man going to the city, expecting to be married. I didn't hear a lot about it, because all this happened before I was born. I know that things didn't turn out like they planned. He disappeared and she came back to the farm, and then Max was born.

I never understood why he was named Max. There were quite a number of Freds, Petes and Franks, but I never knew anyone else named Max. It wasn't even a saint's name, but maybe that didn't make any difference because he was Presbyterian. I don't know what he was like before the accident, because I was only three at the time. I saw a picture once, and he looked cute, just like any other kid. His mother, my aunt Eunice, went downhill fast after he was born. She developed pernicious anemia. There wasn't much they could do for it in those days, in the early twenties. My mother talked about it once in a while, and she got nauseous and disgusted when she described how Eunice was supposed to eat ground raw liver, or at least try to. She couldn't eat enough of it and she died.

Grandma and grandpa adopted Max, so he became Max Miller Rubert. He very much liked belonging to the grandparents, but I think the middle name of Miller made him feel he knew his dad. Later on, when he was about fifteen and I was nine, he decided he was legally my uncle. Next, he came up with the idea that he was my mother's brother. All this seemed to make him feel more important, but it annoyed my mother like everything.

It didn't make much difference to me, so once in a while when I was feeling just right, I called him, "Uncle." I liked Max. We got along most of the time. We worked in the garden together, shocked oats, and walked up and down the graveled road picking up special rocks. Best of all, we went to the pasture in the early morning dew, to bring in the cows. Like I said, I don't know how he was before the accident, but now he didn't laugh a lot. I suppose he looked pretty sour to folks who didn't know him. He also was awkward and clumsy. He just didn't ever do things other kids did, like tell riddles or jokes, or play stunts on people. I was always being asked to recite or do some show-off thing, but Max never was. I don't think he ever won anything like a spelling bee, or hit a home run. Nobody patted his head or praised him except to tell him he was a good worker. He just didn't get good things like kids are supposed to. Being six years older, he really was somewhat like an uncle, and the best thing I could ever do was call him that. Him being older did have some advantage. He told me a lot about girls. I think he must have heard it all from other guys, because I don't think he had ever been close to a real live girl. Anyway, it made interesting listening.

Max wasn't bad looking, but he couldn't forget about his eye. He had some idea how it looked. He could see in the mirror that it was distracting, and he knew it was hard for people to look right at him and try to carry on a conversation. Really, it was mostly a problem when you first started; you didn't know where to look, into his good eye or at the other one that was slightly drifting. I mostly looked at his nose, and after a minute or two I would get going, forget all about it and keep talking right along. The bad eye wasn't so ugly. It wasn't discolored or bloody, or even worse, dead white like a picture I once saw. It moved along with the good one, but it didn't go exactly to the same spot. I think he made a bigger thing of it than necessary. Like I said, after you forgot about it and got talking, he seemed pretty much normal. Unfortunately, he couldn't get past it. He imagined people squirmed when they got stuck to talk with him. He thought they were looking around him for someone else. Then he would walk away and do something different. It was hard to get to know him, or find out what he was all about, when he kept drifting around. Most of the time it wasn't his eye, it was just him. I think I can understand that it would be difficult, getting off to a shaky start, not having your own folks and living with old people, not even having your own name, and not knowing who you are. That would wear on me.

Max went to the school about a mile away, through eighth grade. This was hit or miss depending on the weather and the needs at the farm, but grandma was serious about school, because she had earned a Normal School Certificate and was qualified to teach, although I don't think she ever did. Then Max started high school, but that didn't last. He had to pay for an eight mile ride with older kids who had a big touring car, and were running something of a bus service. I suspect they made fun of him. The ride, and the day at school, took him away from the work at home where he was really needed. He didn't have any school ambitions, so he quit. His classmates in eighth grade were mostly working at home or as hired hands for a dollar a day, and he followed their pattern. Max was smart, in a common sense way. He was good with simple numbers, he could read, and he could fix things, and he worked hard. This was a good combination for a farm boy. He had learned very young that the one thing that got him approval when the flashier boys were showing off, was simply to work harder. He enjoyed sweating. It was proof that he was working hard, and he tended to overdo it, so he looked like he was doing more than maybe he really was. Sometimes he was clumsy and got in his own way. When I got old enough to notice such things, I thought he acted like a puppy, sometimes doing dumb things or getting kind of tangled up, just trying to get attention.

The years passed. Max changed physically, but there was little opportunity on the farm for social life. He became strong, not bulging pretty like the Charles Atlas ads, but work strong. Farm boys used to lift a newborn calf onto their shoulders every day, with the idea that they would get stronger and eventually be able to lift it when it was a full grown cow. Of course, this never worked. They also did a scissor squeeze with their legs on a bag of oats, trying to split it, with the same lack of success. By early summer he had a typical farmer tan, face, neck and arms up to where the sleeves were rolled. By mid-June he was shirt off and full brown. He would never have known it, but from the waist up he would have been a great swimming suit model. He was accepted as a good and steady farmer, one you could exchange a day's work with. Supposedly, grandpa promised him a share of the farm, whatever that meant. I don't think they signed any papers, although that would have made it official and probably satisfied him. Maybe he did get a little more say in how things were done, but I never saw much difference.

When Max was twenty four, he found a young lady who appealed to him. I think they met at the Mt. Pleasant Presbyterian church. Max had a surprisingly good singing voice. With head back, neck veins bulging and voice in full vibrato, he was at his best, and may have overwhelmed her. His rendering of *"Shall We Gather at the River"* was a very compelling invitation. She was a visitor from a nearby small town. She was pretty and quiet, and unlike most of the farm girls, soft-sweet. She worked in an office, and everything about her seemed to be from a different world. To Max she was almost a princess. Surprising to us, and also to Max, she liked him. I was in my second semester of college, at an age when I thought maybe I should give her a closer look. Instead, I was invited to be Max's best man at their wedding. Things were so simple in those days, a dozen people gathered in the front room of her home, a ten minute ceremony with a few preacher words, a dinner, and they were married.

Shortly after that, Grandpa died. One morning after chores and breakfast, he said, "Carrie, I'm going to rest a little before I go to the field," and he laid down for eternity. Grandma and Max stayed on the farm for one season, but grandma was tired, and Max wanted to try a job in town, with a regular weekly paycheck. The farm was sold. Grandma probably kept most of the money, in spite of Max's so-called share. She bought an older house in town and rented rooms. She seemed to enjoy the rest of her life, and at one point, despite her Presbyterian standards, even discovered the simple pleasure of a cocktail.

Max found a job at the meat packing plant. As a farm boy he had some experience with butchering, and working only forty hours a week was almost a vacation, but being inside, and the monotony, got to him, and he quit. Coincidentally, at this time I planned my first novel, and borrowed heavily from the events in his life. In it I called him, "Orrie." This was the name of a neighbor Amish boy, and it gave me the feeling of the simple things of farm life. I was also influenced by the book, **Giants in the Earth,** which we were reading at school. My proposal and outline for this was rejected by a publisher, but I was twenty then and survived.

Max went through a succession of jobs, maintenance man, night watchman, cleaning offices at night, and finally custodian for a church. This was comfortable. He related well to the pastor. He felt that he was part of the team doing the Lord's work, and he had a large ring of keys to enhance his authority. This was the end stage of his development. From then on, he seemed to age faster. He lost the eagerness and simplicity that had carried him past his early limitations. He became morose and increasingly opinionated. His speech was abrasive, and he delivered his words with a take it or leave attitude. Perhaps more typically he used the words of his world: "Like it or lump it." Ruth was still his patient wife, but she no longer had an expanding influence on him. Day after day he upholstered his constricted world with ironclad views, and stayed there, where he was the undisputed master. Suddenly he developed an uncommon malignant disease of the bone marrow and died. Max was a living aphorism, that for want of a nail, a shoe, a horse, a rider, the battle could indeed be lost. In simplistic summary, Max Miller Rubert, for all of his life, was just a half inch away from hitting the mark.

Chapter 7

Camelot Regained

The farm was a place of wonder in the mind of a child. It spread seamless to the edge of mystery, unmarked by roads, and larger than our little town, it stretched to the gateway of once upon a time. In one distant corner was where the giant lived, and in another was the castle of the fairy princess. I wandered free, following butterflies among their friends, past flat-petalled wild roses, over tiny, low blooming woods berries, through misty elfin toad-stool glades. I shared the birthing of opening buds, and tasted windborne nectar.

My pockets bulged with treasure: nuts and bark, a leaf, a twig or seed pod, and agates from a dryrun creek, a vestige from geologic time of a once proud torrential river. Meadowlarks serenaded with their broken song, and hawks, as if appointed to watch over me, spiraled in the thermals. The pastured colts rubbed and nuzzled, then frolicked away, paused and looked back, inviting me to follow. In the puffy high clouds rising above the far hills, I read messages of an Indian greeting. I was at peace and never afraid.

80CR

My ninth birthday had just passed with a disappointing lack of excitement. There was no party, no *"Pin the Tail on the Donkey"* or "*Blind Man's Buff*," and no screaming girls to chase, but grandma really tried. She baked an angel food cake, the special company recipe with thirteen egg whites that she had to beat for about a half an hour. Then she fussed trying to get steady heat in the wood stove oven, using only small uniform pieces of fast burning kindling wood, and constantly adjusting the damper. After she put the cake in the oven, she guarded its door so no one would jar or open it and let in a draft. She walked on tiptoe, even though it was a cement floor, and she whistled under her breath. When she added more wood, she lifted the stove lids as gently as checking the eggs under a setting hen. Finally, she made a seven minute boiled frosting, and let me lick the spoon and the bowl. All of this sure made me know it was my special day.

Unfortunately, grandpa sort of rained on my picnic. He gave me a sharp bone handle pocket knife. This was such a routine tool for a farm boy that I didn't think of it as a real present. I just stuck it into the little side pocket of my overalls and started to walk away. I don't think I even thanked him. He reached out and rubbed my head like he did when he was trying to be fun, and then he gave me a lecture about taking on new work responsibilities, now that I was getting older. He smiled and seemed very happy.

It sounded awful to me. I just didn't understand why things had to change. I never thought there was anything special about being nine. I know that turning thirteen is a big deal, then you're a teenager, but being nine is just automatic. You go to bed at night when you are eight, and you wake up in the morning and are nine. Anyway we didn't really discuss it, and I sure didn't have any vote on it. It was just the ways things were in the country. It was practical, and it must have worked. This older and responsible stuff had been going on for two months since my birthday, and I somewhat got into the idea, and was trying. It was actually a good feeling knowing that grandpa relied on me for some things, and that I was really a help. I knew I soon would be milking and driving the team.

Of all the jobs in my new grown-up world, I liked best going to the dewy pasture in the first gray of morning to bring the cows in for milking. I was alone in my private world. In the waning night, vague shadows awakened and became trees, or lumbered uncertainly and cows took form. It could have been scary, but in all my days at the farm, things were magical and wondrous, and I had never been afraid. Beyond this mystic opening, the day deteriorated into a dulling routine. I missed the aimless frolicking with birdsongs, butterfly aerobatics and breezes flavored with nectar. Those days were lost to busy-work. It had been some time since I last dreamed of a fairy princess or worried about an ogre. Now I was assigned to a responsible role in the real world. I hoed in the garden, gathered eggs, cleaned and greased the plow blades, oiled the harnesses and carried water to the men in the fields. I was increasingly unsure about the worth of growing older and being so busied with trivial realities. In the dawn I could escape, but the rest of the day ground on without excitement until the evening came. This was my next most favorite time.

Then the farm shifted into idle. The cows, relieved of milk, ambled to the pasture, and with stiff legged jerky moves eased down into the soothing grass. Through the night they chewed quietly in their determined habit, renewing themselves for tomorrow. The horses were turned loose, and even the graying mares rejoiced, ran and kicked, then rolled in the dew, erasing the sweat marks of the harness. Pigs lay unmoving in their mud, and grunted softly, digesting the hickory nuts and corn they had foraged throughout the day. The chicken house was closed against a fox or weasel. The dog lay near the porch steps, hind legs twitching, as he coursed in dreams with his wild wolf cousins.

The grownups sat on the swing or the wicker chairs on the lawn, kept treeless so there would be no clutter of leaves. With hands folded they waited for the clock to say they could go to bed. In this routine contentment they spoke softly, and were happy to be together. The night was not just an absence of light; it was a pause when the world held its breath, and in the silence little sounds could be heard that were overwhelmed by the day.

When the moon was round, all the world was silvered. Faces were bright and free of lines and care. When the moon waned and was but a curving sliver, the Milky Way showed itself as a swath spread across the sky, and stars glittered brilliant from the black. We pointed to the Dipper with pride, but this was the limit of our science. Beyond that we could not separate a planet from the suns. Such knowledge might have been helpful in sailing a distant ocean, but in our landlocked lives it did not make the corn grow any better.

Tonight's darkness was near to absolute. At times we only knew that hands attached to the arms by feeling for them. They could not be seen six inches in front of one's face. There was no electricity, and light was not squandered on the outside night. It was carefully conserved within, where a single kerosene lamp sat on the table. This could brighten a room enough to read by close up, but beyond twenty feet it was only a point of flickering yellow. Yet, this tiny flame could be seen across fields between neighboring farms a half mile away. A whipperwill soloed against a background chorus of crickets, and a distant owl challenged menacingly with its insistent "Whoo."

This night, so like all the others, was two months past the longest day, in the middle of the dog days of August. It was without a hint of breeze. I had washed my feet in the horse tank, squishing between my toes the velvet green that grew on the bottom. I was ready for bed. Then someone said, "Wouldn't ice cream taste wonderful, maybe with some berries on it?" I was more awake now. Certainly cousin Max would jump at this chance to use his new driver's license and go in the model T, but not a word. I waited, and fidgeted. I stared at him, but he didn't even look back. Grandpa yawned, and I was afraid he would get up and go to bed, but instead he just gave me a slight nudge with his elbow, like you do with your heels when you want the pony to move. Suddenly, I was startled by my own voice saying, "I'll go". I squeezed my feet into shoes that daily grew tighter as my bare feet calloused and splayed. I took a half dollar from grandpa and headed down the rutted driveway, very slowly. No one offered advice, or even tried to stop me. Perhaps in my subconscious this may have been reassuring, knowing they thought it was something I could do. At the end of the drive I looked back hopefully, then turned right on the graveled road.

I knew that Marsh's General Store was exactly one mile. I had walked it before, but never at night. My shoes were hard against the stones, and made noise too loud in the silence. I thought of taking them off, but they would have been a bother to carry. As I walked on through the canopy of arching trees, now barely visible against the fullness of the night, I pictured in my mind the exciting wonders I would see at the store.

Just inside the door was the big attraction, a wheel of orange cheese, two feet across. Lying next to it was a long knife, like a sword, that I had seen used to cut slices as people ordered it. It looked so sharp that cutting was effortless, even fun. I would have liked to try it, but the nearest I came to sword play was chopping corn stalks. The cheese was a most popular topic on the phone party-line. Someone would give a general ring like they did for a fire or other emergency, and tell all the listeners who answered, "They've got in a new cheese, and it's good." I rehearsed: maybe if I stared at it long enough, and looked sad, I might get a sliver. Next to it was a barrel of herring with little round spices floating on top. I never tried that because it smelled fishy, and I got enough of that from the bullheads we caught in the river. A huge jar of sweet pickles was on the meat display case. They were dark green and little, just about one bite size. All the farm women made pickles, jars and crocks of them, but those were dills and bread and butter chunk kinds. For some reason no one knew how to make sweet pickles that stayed crunchy, so this was a big seller.

The wall shelves were filled with cans and jars of fruits and vegetables, mostly different from the things we grew. The labels were splashes of bright colors, like circus posters, that made our gardens look dull. All around were bags and barrels of sugar and flour and beans and rice, and bins with see-through lids filled with cookies and crackers, even little round ones. At one end of the counter was a machine pretty much like our sausage grinder, but it was used for coffee. I was disappointed that anything that smelled so exciting could taste so bitter awful. Next to it was a more enjoyable apparatus that ground out paste from peanuts. This tasted great, but it stuck to your teeth something terrible. At the candy counter, which I knew best of all, were rows of glass containers, some standing slantwise with hinged lids or others like vases with pointy lids. They looked like getting ready for Christmas, filled with colorful jawbreakers, hoarhound or lemon drops, marshmallow peanuts, cinnamon hearts, licorice sticks, pink and white mints the size of checkers and much more. It was a place to stand and dream about having enough money to get sick.

I looked ahead and saw a light mounted above the front door. Electricity had come this far into the country and was promised soon for everyone. It was a taste of another world. I hadn't seen the store lighted before, but I was happy that the distance seemed less now. As I walked, I practiced what I would do. I went in. Everything was arranged pretty much as I had previewed it, but more exciting with all the lights. It was a carnival of yearning. The cheese was up front as big as ever. It was covered with a glass dome that gave it a special quality, unavailable except to the privileged ones. Mr. Marsh was sitting with two men smoking and talking. He wasn't a natural smiler, and I knew he didn't like kids. I stood as tall as I could trying to look older. Even for penny candy he made you show your money first, so I held out my half dollar and said, "Mr. Marsh, I'd like a quart of vanilla ice cream, hand packed, if you please." His face let me know I had bothered him, but he got up and walked to the back of the store toward the cooler. I followed him. After all, it was my money. He opened the huge door, much like the brown varnished one on the ice box at home, and then he walked through it. I peeked around him, but all I could see were blocks of ice covered with sawdust. "You want to come in?" I did.

It was heavenly cool. He took a cardboard carton with flap covers and a wire handle and fitted it into a metal frame of the same size and shape. Then he began stuffing chunks of ice cream into it that he dug out of a big tub with a scoop. I wouldn't have believed there was that much ice cream in the whole county. He kept packing it in, really leaning on it. That must have been the reason for the metal frame, so it wouldn't split. What started out as wonderful began to look like real work. He even grunted a time or two. He knew grandma would call and yell at him if it wasn't right. I could just hear her, "We're not paying for air, you know." He folded the flaps and handed it to me. It must have weighed five pounds. So this is what *handpacked* means, I thought.

I walked out into the night. It was so very much darker in contrast to the electric show inside, and looking down the road, the black was more dense than on the way in, like I couldn't walk through it. The road had been empty then; now it was lonely, and looked as long as forever. I turned left. I knew that was the way. The lighted area around the store front ended within fifty feet, and was replaced by the unknown. The gravel underfoot was familiar and I could just follow that home. I headed away from the light, very unwilling. After a few minutes I looked back. The light was small and covered with a swarm of bugs. I walked faster. I knew there was a cemetery on the left. Of course it was there on the way in, but the pictures in my mind had blocked it out, and I hadn't really noticed. Now I was passing the gate. I knew it wasn't scary. We often visited there on Sunday after church to say a quiet hello to aunt Eunice and grandma Smith who were resting there, but this was different. The markers stood out of the black ever so faintly, maybe like gray ghosts. I ran.

When I settled to a walk, I heard the scrunching of small things in the undergrowth, falsely secure in the leaves and the dark, but the owls could see, and nothing was safe. Were there owls large enough to take an interest in me? Their "Whoo" raised goose-pimples as I pondered this question. If not owls, then possibly bats. They were fast and invisible in the dark. I wished I had worn a hat, because it was a known fact that bats got in your hair and tangled so tight they had to be cut out.

Low breathing and snuffling followed along where the fence should be. Those were big animals, and they knew I was here. Of course they could see in the dark, otherwise they would run into things. Louder crashings, horses I hoped, or could it be the bull? The neighbor's bull was loose in their pasture, and last week it treed the hired man who went to bring in the cows. A fence is just weathered posts and strands of rusty wire. Mostly a flimsy marker to show people how far they own. The gentle farm animals, used to the smell of people, had accepted fences as part of their world and limits. They fitted into the cycle of work and rewards, but the bull didn't live by those rules. Was he eying me and pawing the ground?

Grandpa once told me Red Riding Hood's wolf lived in a corner of the farm next to the ogre, but that was in the days when I still played in fairy tales. Later, he told me that wasn't quite true. They were all gone before he bought the farm twenty years ago. He sounded very sure of that.

I looked back. The store light was barely visible, just a flicker as the tree branches waved in and out of the way. It seemed as small as when I first saw it on my way going. That must mean I was getting near home. At a clearing between woods, on one side I saw a small wavering light. I thought it was a lamp, but could I be turned around, and that was the direction of the store? I panicked. Would I recognize the farm when I got there? Would a lamp on the table be enough? Could I have walked past it?

The neighbors beyond had a large dog I didn't want to meet in the dark. Should I turn around and go back to the store and ask for help? It probably was closed now. A dog yipped and jumped at me. It was my very own Buddy. He was just white enough to be visible. I yelled toward the light, "Grandpa, is that you?"

"Bobby, is the ice cream melted?" I had forgotten it, but it was clutched in my hands and felt firm and cold. I gave it to grandma. Her question sounded like she was close to guessing the truth.

"You made good time. Did you run all the way?" She moved to dish it up.

I had no taste for it and didn't feel like talking. I said quietly, "I'm tired. I think I'll just go to bed."

Grandpa took my hand and carried the lamp as we walked to bed. He scratched my back until I almost purred. "Bobby, maybe we tried too hard. You did good, but you go on being a boy, be eight for little while longer, and let me be just be your grandpa, and remember it that way always."

In a deeper plane, far below numbers and years, I had a sense of having aged, at least enough to know the torment of dark imaginings, but with unreasoned denial I snuggled into the downy cool beneath an angel's wing, closed out the night, and once again, as a child, slept in peace.

Chapter 8

My Baseball Mitt

I had a catcher's mitt. I don't know where it came from. Maybe my father bought it, but that wasn't the usual thing to do in those days. Things just appeared from a shelf or a trunk or an old box in a neighbor's shed. They were "Handed on," as the people used to say. I was about seven or eight, and just beginning to play ball. Of course, it was baseball because the sissy game of Softball and underhand pitching hadn't caught on yet. In fact, it never did in Iowa, as much as I know.

Do you know what a catcher's mitt is? Well, it is big. It looked like a pillow strapped on my eight year old hand. It was dull gray, probably just worn off from being brown. There was a deep cup recess in the center, and the trick was to hammer your fist into this to make a loud smacking sound, while you yelled at the pitcher, real or imaginary, "Burn it in there."

The glove was leather, of course, because nothing else was tough enough. Plastic sure hadn't been invented. It was part of the routine to oil the glove after every use, whether it was a big game or just catching a few to warm up the pitcher. Neat's foot oil was the best. It was absolutely necessary. Everyone knew that, or as my mother always said whenever I asked her, "Why," about anything, "It's a known fact". We dazzled each other with lots of this secret boy-type knowledge. Do you know what a neat is? Everybody knew what that was in my day. A neat is some kind of a fly, and we spent a lot of time sitting around oiling and spitting, wondering how they ever caught enough flies, and even a bigger problem, how did they separate off the feet. This was pretty important stuff that only guys would know. If you told anyone who wasn't to be trusted, like girls or your mom, you'd be classed as a "Wigger," and there was nothing worse. Anyway, this was absolutely the best, so anyone caught with the smell of lard or machine oil on his glove was in deep trouble. The oil really did a lot to improve the looks of my muddy gray mitt; it became almost shiny black, for a while.

Eventually the seams began to wear and separate, and I could see that the mitt was stuffed with horsehair. It was packed tight so it would be a good cushion for the hand, that is everywhere except in the center where the cup was. There the front and back layers of leather met. That was all that covered your palm, and it sure wasn't enough to handle the smoke when the pitcher really got going. You just learned to squeeze your hand a little to tighten the pocket, and then you caught the ball kind of on the rim. This sometimes didn't work, because if you were too chicken, you made the cup too small and the ball just bounced off.

I was the only one in the neighborhood with a catcher's mitt so it made me special. I had to be the catcher. This was big. I was next most important after the pitcher, but this show off spot had its downside. You had to squat close behind the batter all the time, while other guys out in the field were horsing around and showing off for the girls. There was also a chance that you could get hit in the face, or someplace worse, by a ticked ball.

I survived all this, but me and my mitt were just sort of a necessity. I knew I really wasn't awful good, and they mostly just put up with me because my glove gave the team a look of class. Deep down I knew this wasn't important. What I loved most was playing catch with my father. It was one of the few things we did together. Then he got sick the next year and we never played again.

Chapter 9

The Long Shadow

Jesup, Iowa, where I lived the first years of my life, was a town of about six hundred people. It was like a thousand others scattered across the country. The Illinois Central ran through, but no one was concerned about who lived on which side of the tracks. There wasn't a bad one, or for that matter, a good one either. The creamery was the most prominent operation in town, and got more publicity than anything else. Jesup butter was the source of our pride. It was in fierce competition with Dike and Benson, but these were just crossroad creameries that didn't have the same important city backing. We were known for a radius of at least three or four counties. This may not sound like much in today's world, but in the 1930's in rural Iowa, you settled for any little thing, and made something out of nothing. There wasn't a Chamber of Commerce promoting us. This was Small Town America before Norman Rockwell defined how it should be.

Things were predictable, and life was more or less asleep, but one day of the year, in late August, Jesup exploded. That was Farmer's Day. It was so perfectly, meaningfully named. This was the only Saturday of the year when the farm folks hustled through the morning chores, forgot about the fields, blocked out the ever-present concerns about the animals, put on new overalls or aprons and bonnets, and took off to town for the entire day. It was a mass migration, and the town swelled to a few thousand.

Of first importance was the tall corn contest. This was the symbol that represented the state in song and folklore, and more recently, the logo on license plates. In a good growing season the winning entry could exceed fourteen feet. The 4H clubs paraded calves and young heifers, previewing the promise of increased milk and butterfat production. Church auxiliaries set up striped tent dining halls, and outdid each other with their offerings of four meats and homemade cakes and pies. It was a showcase for the kitchen-bound women, and on this day they sparkled and beamed, and reveled in their recognition.

In the afternoon a baseball game determined the unofficial county champion. After this, evening chores still had to be done, so someone from each farm rushed home to do a halfhearted job of milking and feeding the animals. Everyone reassembled for the evening boxing matches. There was a proper roped ring, and a referee and a loud gong. This was an opportunity for the more rambunctious young men to show off, and established something of a peck order for the coming year.

More exciting than the farm type things was the carnival. There was a girlie show that provided many a farm boy his first glimpse of female parts that at home were carefully hidden by baggy skirts and ample aprons. Farm boys were strong. They played a game of hoisting a newborn calf on their shoulders, and every day they did this with the hope they would get stronger as the calf grew, and finally they would be able to lift a full grown cow. Of course it never worked. They also did a stunt, squeezing a sack of oats in a leg scissor hold, trying to pop it, with the same lack of success. These things were nothing compared to the Charles Atlas looking men on stage who lifted heavy weights, and bridged across two chairs, with a flat rock on their belly. Then they invited people from the audience to try to break it with a sledge hammer. Most of the volunteers were too afraid of hurting them. Freaks were exploited by the insensitive barkers. There were fat ladies and bearded ladies, Siamese twins joined at the hip, which you couldn't really see, and a reptile man with awful scaly skin. There were rides that weren't quite as wild as those at the county fair, but still a lot more exciting than bumping along in a hay wagon.

Finally, there was a fortune teller. This was where I met Prince Riza. He stood tall and mysterious on the stage in front of a tent that was partly covered by a diagram of a head. On this was printed a map of the brain, with the areas involved with Love and Success labeled in red. The Prince wore a white turban edged in gold. It was the first one I had seen in real life. He was demonstrating his power to read minds, and to know things that were hidden from the sight of ordinary men. He spoke slowly in a slightly accented voice, with compelling effect. His gestures were expansive and exaggerated, those of an actor. He held a deck of cards at arm's length in front of himself, cards facing the crowd. He passed one hand over his eyes, as if looking deep into his soul, then announced, not just identified, but announced the card with a ringing tone and a sense of grand triumph. Again, he reached the pack behind him, paused, extended his arms in front, made a symbolic, but apparently essential pass over his eyes, and again announced the newly displayed card.

Each time this was repeated, the wide-eyed farm faces were entranced. They gasped and murmured. There may have been an occasional doubter, but very soon the crowd was ready to be invited into the tent for a personal reading, a demonstration of clairvoyance and a peek through the veil of the future. These were words and ideas not commonly used on the farm. I had seen Grandpa Frank do a trick with a dollar bill, but he needed a special envelope to put it in and make it disappear. It wasn't anything as mysterious as this. Suppose the Prince really could know the future. A line formed quickly to enter the tent. A five minute visit cost one dollar. I had to see him. I clutched my twenty five cents. Maybe he would see me for one minute. I had just one question: would my father die?

I was just nine years old. Boys my age normally were involved with baseball, marbles and pocket knives, but these things had been pushed aside completely by a disaster in my life. My father had been diagnosed as having TB. I scarcely knew what that meant, but it overshadowed and distorted everything in our world. My parents were in turmoil. They floundered through a succession of issues, anguishing over decisions, but actually making very few. Most choices just closed off, and they did whatever was necessary.

My father closed his dental practice, sold the chair to a barber and took down the unusual globe light on which he had proudly painted his name. He arranged to transfer his patients to other dentists, but there weren't many in the area. Mother tried to organize the records and made an attempt to send out bills. This was awkward and painful. No one did that in a small town. The custom was for patients to drop off a chicken or eggs, or vegetables or a load of firewood. Occasionally they might even give a few dollars. That was proper etiquette; getting a statement was unfriendly. Unfortunately, the regular rules didn't solve the problem. Money was needed in a very short time. There was talk of moving. Eventually we did move to grandpa's farm and lived one summer in a tent. It saved rent money, and it also provided the best treatment known for TB, fresh air. It was almost a fun thing to do, but it didn't bring a cure.

After lots of letter writing, and help from the congressman, it was established that the tuberculosis might have come from the time father served as a dentist in the army. The Veteran's Administration conceded that he was: "Ten percent totally disabled." No one understood what that meant, not even the doctors at the VA hospital. It didn't produce much of a pension, I think it was $27.00 a month. He tried staying at the hospital but he couldn't do it. He was too lonely and frightened. There were no clear answers as to what was the best thing to do. The shock and confusion were too fresh for reliable decisions.

Now I was going to get an answer. I waited in line, at the very end. Whenever someone came behind me, I went behind him, because I thought if there wasn't anyone with a dollar, the Prince might take me for my quarter. Finally he called me in. He looked tired, much less shining and all-knowing than he did on the platform. He spoke softly, without an accent, as he greeted me. I blurted, "I don't have the full price, just a quarter, but that should pay for one minute. Just one question, my father has TB; will he die?" As he looked at me, he seemed very intense, but somehow soft and gentle. After a long pause, when I didn't know if he was really thinking about my question, he leaned close and said in a low voice, "He will be with you a long time." He got up and went into the backroom. He didn't even take my quarter.

I felt a sudden lift. This was what I wanted to hear. He hadn't said "He will die", but he didn't say he would get well. I repeated his exact words as I left the tent. Then I sagged. I saw a pile of dirty clothes in a corner. This was the reality. The whole thing was just a stunt. It was a junky carnival, it was trashy, and he was just an ordinary man. He didn't know anything more than other people. The good feeling was gone. I ran home crying, hoping no one would see me in the early darkness. I found my father in a coughing spasm, smoking a cigarette.

ଈଓଷ

My father died when I was fourteen, but we had been lost to each other since I was seven. We had very little meaningful and memorable time together, certainly not enough to give me a sense of his ways and values. Most of what I know is anecdotal, and as hearsay, is probably unreliable. My personal, real memories are few, but the rarity has just increased their value, and they are enough to build on with creative fancy. Unfortunately, without a pole image, I have stumbled at times, trying to be a perfect father.

My father is mostly a montage of faded pictures, showing a boy throwing a baseball or duded out in the styles of the early twenties, posed with mother's family, bedecked with furs and big hats. His own family was more reticent, or perhaps just too Germanic for that kind of time waste, so pictures with them are very sparse. My favorite is the studio portrait, an oval head and shoulders, with probably thirty or more similar young men, in his Creighton College of Dentistry graduating class. It was elegant. He wore a white bow tie and a wing tip collar, and exuded youthful pride and confidence. I was told that originally he had enrolled in the medical school, but after some undefined conflict with the professor of Anatomy, he switched to the Dental school. As incidental or trivial as this was, mother often speculated how different things might have been had he not made this change. Certainly, it seems a disastrous whim of fate. Much less appealing was the picture of him in the Anatomy lab, poised over a cadaver, in the process of dissecting and examining some minute structure. It was calculated to show that these students were privy to hidden ghoulish wisdom, beyond the ken of average men. It is a vivid, but unpleasant memory, and very unwieldy to work into the full dimensional tapestry of a loved one. I threw it away.

After graduation, he entered the Army as a first lieutenant in the Dental Corps. His rank in the Army meant very little to anyone, but it provided one of my most enduring memories. Every Decoration day, as Memorial day was then called, as the ranking member of the local veterans' group, he marched his men to the cemetery for the solemn ceremony of firing a volley over the graves of those killed in the war. He was as erect as five feet six inches can get, in flared riding pants, polished leather puttees, Sam Browne belt and high visored bill cap. His command, "Present arms! Ready! Fire!" excited me.

None of my five year old friends had anything like this. When the soldiers left, I scurried around gathering all the cartridge cases I could find. They were great for trading. His military career was in reality something short of heroic. He served as a dentist for a brief time. It was soon discovered that he had gone to secretarial school before Dental school and was a skilled typist and knew shorthand. He was transferred, and became the secretary for the commanding general of Ft. Oglethorpe, and didn't touch a dental drill until after the Armistice. This bit of information surfaced quite incidentally. When I was in high school, the Underwood company sponsored a demonstration by a speed typist. He typed to music and did cute rhythm bits, and then showed off how easily the machine performed as he typed one hundred words a minute. When I replayed this wonderment at home, my father said that before he entered Dental School he could type one hundred ten words a minute, and was offered a job by the Underwood company. Another meager memory.

Chapter 10

Regret

The most deeply felt poem I have written was lost. When I was sixteen, still in the shadow of my father's death, I wrote some very sentimental, rhymed verses. They were undoubtedly maudlin, but expressed so intensely the spirit of my life, that I forgave myself for the overindulgence. I wrote in a rather good script, that is for a future physician, on lined, three hole paper. It was certainly not elegant, but I made copies for Mother and a few folks who might read it. At one point in college, in a Freshman English course, I turned it in as an assignment. I have a terse note from the professor that it lacked "a feeling of intellectual reality." Whatever that means, it was as much feeling as this young person could force onto paper. It was published in a rather limited printing; years later Mother submitted it to the nursing home newsletter. Then it was lost, surviving only as a fragmented memory, but as such, it was safe from critical scrutiny. It acquired a patina, and an aura of how great it might have been. In unplanned time it surfaced in some archive, probably a prayer book. It still recalls the pain of those simple days. It was written in 1937.

Ode To My Father

My Fathers who art in Heaven,
For I now have two up there,
From the child of your creation,
Listen to his prayer.

GOOD GENES, LUCK, LOTS OF PRAYERS

O God, what have I done or left undone,
What karma can this be,
That my father should be taken
Before he could speak to me.

For seven years we lived, together yet apart,
Divided by walls and self-restraint.
We lived and loved and cared for him,
But we were fearful of his taint.

We knew this earth was not his home.
And knowing this we drained each hour
Of all the good it had in store,
As fruits stolen from eternity's bower.

But the time was fast approaching
When You began to see
That without my father there with you,
Heaven could not a heaven be.

We watched his losing fight for life,
Life which rarely had been kind,
But kind or cruel, we would still be here,
So he was loathe to leave us behind.

His sweats, his pains, his prayers,
Must still be incense in the sky,
But Almighty, you would have him near,
And we saw him kiss his cross and die.

GOOD GENES, LUCK, LOTS OF PRAYERS

We did not need the doctor's words.
We felt his soul take flight.
We did not see an angel host
Or a blinding flash of light.

But now the room was cold and still.
His suffering was done.
And all could see this was not
Our once beloved one.

What marks this change from life to death?
Atheist, answer if you can.
Does not the body still remain,
But whence has gone the man?

We made his bed a funeral pyre.
And burned the mat on which he had lain.
The consuming unrelenting fire,
Rendered to heaven his oblation of pain.

Father, you never taught me much by word
The things that I should know.
You showed me rather by your death
Which paths of life to go.

My father who art in Heaven,
The one I never knew,
I can do naught but live and pray,
That I may come to you.

Chapter 11

Esther

No one can visit a nursing home, and come away without being changed. It isn't possible to be casual about it. All of the certainty that exuded from the young and the healthy, so unconsciously taken for granted, is lost, sopped up by the vacuum of aging. In youth the fuel tank was full of unlimited vigor. The gauge stayed at the top, seemingly forever, and needed no tending. Then, unobserved it slowly began a downward drift, and suddenly, with jarring impact, it is fluttering on empty. The change is palpable. We now have a subset stuck in ante-mortem dormancy. The air is an almost particulate fog of cooking smells, medicines, bedpans and worn bodies. It overwhelms the ventilator filters. Incidental intruders, delivery people, the mail man, repair and service personnel, hurry in and out, almost holding their collective breath, hoping not to catch something. Even the doctors wash their hands more often. Nurses are forced friendly, over-brimming and busy with little things to keep themselves distracted. Only the aides, so close in personal contact, have come to terms with the raw reality, and are free to be themselves. Enlightened social workers, those professionals charged with putting a cosmetic face on all of this, are busy leading group activities, exercises for the wheelchair bound, or issuing funny hats, and conducting the kazoo band for a birthday party that the honored guest doesn't know is happening. Children visit and share their kittens and puppies, because they are supposed to be soothing to the "residents." High school choral groups excel at entertaining them. Unfortunately, the beneficiaries of this good feeling and pretense are those who have done it, not the aged victims. All this activity is designed to be very reassuring to the relatives.

All but the most infirm are assembled in the day room. This is a meaningless euphemism. It is really the store room, where people are herded and parked like study hall, so one sharp-eyed monitor can keep track of a larger number than in the individual rooms or side hallways. It is the ultimate display of the spectrum of dysfunction and disarrangement possible in the human condition. Visitors stake out a quiet corner with their special one, as they strive for a meaningful exchange that will bring them together again on a plane that used to be.

Esther did not fit this pattern. She was unchangingly coiffed and finished. Her iron gray hair was positioned in a parallel series of marcelled waves, day after day the same, as if she wore a wig that was carefully transferred between her head and a mold on the dresser. She wore lipstick much too bright for the setting. Her dresses most frequently were floral and positive. Dominating this were chocolate-pudding eyes that arrested your attention. She was not an inert part of the background scenery. Her voice was louder than normal, proportional to her hearing loss. It was measured, and precisely projected, a nagging reminder to me of her injunction throughout my boyhood, "modulate your voice." This was the self image and persona she chose to present to the public. It hid the real world of her daily living. Our brief visits made only aliquot samplings of the range of her experiences, of the fears and the little pleasures, and the long emptiness of each day and week. The loved one we treasure is a patchwork projection of remembered mannerisms, anecdotes, interests, accomplishments and conflicts, and love. It is a fabrication that takes on a reality of more substance than the troubled and fragile one we know in this real world.

GOOD GENES, LUCK, LOTS OF PRAYERS

ℰᏫℭᏒ

Mother, or Grandma Esther, is a potpourri of vivid images. Going to Grandma's for Thanksgiving or Christmas dinner is a standard of American nostalgia. Not quite so with Grandma Esther. It wasn't the trip or the quality of the food; it was the challenge of surviving the adventure. The hot chocolate and delicate grated pecan cookies in the late evening, were an ideal reward after our train trip on the Land of Corn, but the traditional family meat loaf was a surprise each time, as she endlessly revised the recipe until she destroyed it. The last version was full of oat meal and chopped up Rath's breakfast sausages. The dinners at the Elks club, where she was something of a doyenne, gave full expression to how unpleasant she could be. The chicken livers were inevitably underdone or burned and too crisp. Dinners at Bishop's cafeteria stretched over many years, and we endured the deterioration of the food and service, long before she recognized how bad it had become. In a Chinese restaurant, declaring that Grandpa Leo loved mustard, she slathered his egg rolls with the blistering sauce, which he ate with tears in his eyes rather than argue. At a newly opened oriental palace, whose name translated into *"House of Peace,"* we encountered a Kung Fu demonstration with live cleavers. This spilled over from the kitchen, and the patrons fled in panic. With her diminished hearing, Grandma had difficulty understanding all the commotion. She did not share the feeling of being threatened, and simply asked if we couldn't go someplace for pizza. We recall her habit of clearing the central table area by pushing the salads farther and farther to the side, and the time (every one knew it would inevitably happen) one fell to the floor at the airport dining room. And the time she dumped the bowl of hot liquid strawberry Jello onto her new kitchen carpet, and then frantically mopped and vacuumed before it hardened into the nubby nylon. Dinners with Grandma had little to do with the traditional seasonal smells and trappings. Each time was something different We also remember her dominating routine of grooming Grandpa Leo and combing his hair before launching him to work, as he peacefully submitted, then intercepting him on his return home and insisting he remove his shoes. We cringe at the memory of conversations that ended in the prim reprimand, "Your antecedent isn't clear." This pedantic role was her favorite self image, and she glowed when someone would ask if she had been a teacher.

In the mellowing days of her sovereignty, Mother organized her world into controlled simplicity. Like a blind person, with a mind's diagram of each obstacle, she had positioned everything and everybody in stereotyped categories. She reigned by the force of the unexpected, keeping everyone off balance. Our exchanges were something like a visit with a Tourette victim. She delivered seemingly tangential comments, terse and startling; her sentences were abrupt, adjectives were short and verbs were imperatives. On reflection, we usually conceded that they were accurate and fitting, just uncomfortable.

Her nursing home domain was inhabited by class labels instead of individuals. Most of the residents she had dismissed as "funny," meaning a second childhood. A few select ones were wealthy, a word that had a delicious voluptuous feeling for her. She accorded them envious respect. The aides were black and fat. She quickly assured us, and herself, that they were friends and she was never afraid of them.

"Oh, my no, I have always gotten along well with the coloreds." Her roommate, Mrs. Feinberg —Ruby to her — "is Jewish, as you could tell, but she is the nicest lady, not loud and pushy like some of them." Across the hall sitting peacefully in a wheelchair, was a glowing red beehive hairdo. Esther declared for our enlightenment that it was dyed, "Henna , you know." The social workers and assorted therapists were darlings, her very best friends. Each of these pronouncements was made in a casual, non-judgmental manner, in the presence of the individual, as blithely as if she weren't there. If we squirmed and offered a word of defense to deflect or soften the abrasive impact, or Heaven forbid, if we presented a contrary opinion, she closed the discussion with her peremptory, "It's a known fact." Then she would smile indulgently, as at a wayward child, which she considered us still to be. All was forgiven and peace was restored. Again, her black and white world was serene.

Our family was capsulized simplistically, without favored treatment. Each time we visited, the nurses were summoned to meet me, perhaps for the tenth time.

"This is my son, the doctor." Mary was my wife, and a darling nurse. In descending order, our children were labeled. Larry, the crown prince, was the one who wrestled, Steve was taller and played basketball, Mary Beth was a girl and took ballet lessons, and John, undistinguished, was simply eight. These were one dimensional cutouts that served her well in keeping track of a changing cast, that only appeared now and then. We were amused that these labels endured throughout the years in her mind, with very little change, but we realized that we also had developed our own loving pet names with even less logic or meaning. Larry was Peever, Steve was Neenie or Squanto, Mary Beth was Bup, and John, of course, was John Boy. Certainly, we had not improved on Mother's classification, but to the present they have remained full of feeling for us.

Eventually, great-grandchildren were presented to her, but they had little meaning beyond cute and wonderful. They lacked reality, and were more or less incidental, like walk-on props. When our visits came to an end, and it was time to leave town, Mother brought out a little sprinkler bottle of Holy Water and blessed us on our way.

One time an irreverent youngster asked, "Grandma, are you a

priest?"

She smiled tolerantly and said, "No, but I am sacred."

This is the composite, real, three dimensional person who has survived death and lives in our memories intact, not as a sterile, perfect artifact polished by the passing years. We have laughed and cried, and forgiven her, and put her name at the top of our list for canonization.

Chapter 12

Gerontion Updated

On good days I only ache;
Other times I hurt.
Subtle declension of pain
learned from years of creeping age.
An aide pats me, without feeling,
wipes me off and takes the tray,
professionally cool and pleased
that she was not mean.
I am expected to complain:
the food is dull, the service slow,
but I behave, a bit afraid.
They are at times surprised
to discover I have wit,
was once alive, sometimes interesting,
and I was even loved.
But where is the one I used to be?
Now, only a first name
with no distinctive flavor.
No successes follow me here.
Lost in generic old age,
I am a problem not worth solving.

Brief visitors wash their hands on leaving,
then aim a flat smile at the nurse,
content with doing their Christian duty.
Our continuum goes on,
regressing to a common protoplasmic pool,
idling in ante-mortem purgatory,
with the meter running.
No one learns from the aged now.
Like the forest, when an ancient topples
unheard, did it really make a sound,
or any difference?

Chapter 13

Still Water Runs Deep

"You ask what irritates me? It's interesting that you should start with that because I was just thinking about it on my way here. I really don't get angry, and there are very few things that upset me. For instance, the traffic this morning was just wild, probably because it's Friday and everyone is ready for the weekend. Of course there was this young blonde in a little red car, cutting in and out like she owned the road, and, you know, her directional signals must have been broken. She almost clipped me, and I leaned on the horn, but it didn't really annoy me. It's such a shame she was so thoughtless, but actually all she was thinking about was her phone call. Now some people would probably get all excited, but I didn't. I just stayed calm.

"Another example, to show you what I mean, yesterday I was in line at the check out counter. It was the Express, *'Cash Only, 10 Items or Less'.* Wouldn't you know, there was this young woman, the one with the pants that looked like they were painted on, and so much makeup that you just wanted to get a washcloth and scrub her face, she had just unloaded almost a full cart, probably thirty things, lots of chips and junk she didn't need. I thought she would probably have food stamps. She looked like that kind, but no, she pulled out a check book and acted so cool, like she hadn't seen the sign, but she just didn't care. Then she started to write. She held the pen in her fist, clumsy like, and everyone knew she was having trouble with those long purple nails getting in the way. I knew they were artificial, and

I wanted to tell her they were ugly, but it wouldn't have made any difference to her kind. Then the check out girl had to call someone to ok the check. What she really should have done was tell her 'This is an express line, no checks. See the sign?' Of course she didn't do it. I told her so when it was my turn, and that she should have made her load the stuff and go to another lane. I suppose it's hard to find good help to work at a job like that. All the people in line were mumbling, and I knew I had done them a favor. I didn't make a fuss. I just stayed calm and kept my voice even.

"Wouldn't you know it, with all that commotion, I forgot to get extra quarters for the washing machine. My wife won't do the bed sheets in our machine because it overloads it and would wear it out too soon. She wasn't happy. She was going to play bridge, so I had go to the next door liquor store for the quarters, and then take the sheets to the corner laundromat. It never fails to happen. Someone had left a load in the oversize machine, and I had to go back three times. The second time, I left a note that I was going to dump the stuff in a chair. I didn't know if that did any good, but at least it was empty when I returned. Laundromats are always so cluttered, with papers and torn magazines scattered over the floor. While I was sitting there—I wait, you know, so I won't tie up the machine after its done, like someone thoughtlessly did to me—this woman came in with three kids. They were chewing and sucking on some sticky purple stuff, and got it all over their faces. I moved three times to keep from getting smeared. They were whining and fidgeting, and sliding around on the dirty floor. The mother didn't even try to control them, but you knew she couldn't have even if she wanted to. She just wasn't a fit parent. I notice little things like she didn't have a wedding ring, and I knew she was one of those welfare types that just has kids to make money. I couldn't wait to get out of there.

"When I got home, of course my wife was gone playing bridge

and I had to make a peanut butter sandwich. This didn't bother me, I just took it in stride. That's the way I was raised, to accept, adjust and make do, and always see the good in any situation. Mother would never let me get mad. She made me a perfect gentleman. Oh, for heaven's sake, did you say my time is up? Well, I'll see you next week. By the way, doctor, if you want me to continue on the white and blue striped capsules, I'll need a new prescription."

ℴ)ℛ

"Well that's pretty much the way it was in my earlier years, that is before I got married at forty three. By that time I had run out of money, and anyway my wife was helping me. I know I benefited a great deal from the sessions, but I couldn't understand what exactly the doctor did. He just sat there while I talked. Occasionally, he opened his eyes and wrote something down in his folder, probably when I said something he thought was especially profound that maybe he could use for one of his problem patients. I do know that I really did get new insights into what life and people were all about. It has helped me a lot in my job. You see I am the assistant director of employee benefits in the Personnel Department of the local meat packing company. There are many challenging problems with this group because they aren't very sensitive, and it requires all of my deep understanding to keep things going smoothly.

"Over the years I have changed. I know that even I am allowed to get upset, yes even almost angry. I have learned a few strong words. I suppose if I was still talking with the doctor, he would be surprised, and maybe think I was making progress. I do know that I am not always happy with the way things turned out. I used to be very calm, and as mother wanted, a gentleman. Now I have conflicts and frustrations, and I don't know what to do about them. I am almost like other people. Something I have never admitted to anyone, let alone to myself, is that I don't like being small. It is something in my genes, and there isn't anything that can be done about it. In spite of Mother's objection, I worked in a factory when I was going to college, and I got pretty strong. I also lifted a little dumbell I found at a garage sale, and I squeezed a little rubber ball regularly, so I built up good looking arms. I could even tear a deck of cards in two. This impressed the girls, and made the big guys think twice, but do you know, it didn't really do much for me. I still feel short. I also got carpal tunnel problems from all my exercise, and had to have surgery on my wrists. In quiet moments when I talk to myself, I think it may have been a blessing that I wasn't six feet two and two hundred pounds, because then I might have been hostile and even violent."

Chapter 14

Richard

I am four years older than my brother. I don't have any memory of the excitement that his arrival must have generated. I had been the sole focus of parental love during those four years, but contrary to common wisdom, I don't recall any feelings of having been displaced when he joined the family. This may be just a poor memory, or perhaps intentional suppression. I doubt if I was as benign and guiltless as this suggests.

My mother occasionally reminded me of my true nature by describing her horror when she saw me one day leaning over the baby with a large pair of scissors, as if I intended to drop them, point down.

In most of my memories of those earliest days, I loved him very much. Richard was the favored one. He was cute and winsome. The neighbor ladies loved him, and he collected all the cookies. I don't have any memory of jealously, but two years after his birth it was discovered that my father had tuberculosis, and that problem unified us in anxiety and dominated every aspect of our lives. I have the feeling that I was older than the actual difference in our ages. I started in the first grade a year after he was born. I was out of the house, and on my own course, and didn't have much to do with his babyhood. One very powerful bond was a shared bed in the unheated attic. The rafter nails were coated with frost. We huddled together for survival.

GOOD GENES, LUCK, LOTS OF PRAYERS

Our lives were quite separate. The four years gap was just enough for us to be in different stages of interest and activity. By the time we were in high school, it was the difference between a senior and a freshman. Father died when I was fifteen and Richard was eleven. Without any formal declaration I became the man in the family. I don't know if I was any kind of model or male image for him, but I did take care of him. I did some of the cooking and housework, because mother worked in a department store. I also gave unwanted advice.

In high school, I was involved in everything — from student council, school newspaper, and dramatics to wrestling and being a cheerleader. I was a good student. It probably was annoying, even intimidating, for Richard to follow this performance. He was not interested in school, neither the academic nor the extracurricular activities.

I have often thought that he decided he would just ignore the whole thing and reject it as having little value, rather than be in my shadow. I was in college when he graduated from high school. He had a job pumping gas. In those days one didn't do this for himself.

I remember one crucial day that determined the course of his life. I told him I had registered him for the placement exams that were to be given the next week. I suggested that I take him with me to college and show him around. He said emphatically No, he was not interested. This was not discussable. He was defiant. I don't know if he ever looks back on that decision with an awareness of how different his life might have been. I have ever since felt a responsibility, and guilt, for having overwhelmed him. Years later he had rationalized this as it being necessary for him to work and care for mother while I was getting an education.

Richard was an appealing young man, smart and energetic. He was an easy talker and related well to everyone. He was just not academic. The Rath Meat Packing company was the largest employer in our town. I had worked there during college. It was natural that Richard would also go there. He was accepted into the salesman training program. This was a natural for him. He was a shining light, proud and swinging. He was first assigned as a vacation replacement, and traveled across the country, from upstate New York to Denver and Utah. These were brief, two or three weeks in various cities, serving the customers during the vacation absence of their regular salesman. It was an adventure for a young man. He carried with him his special pool cue, and spent hours imitating Minnesota Fats. Somehow he resolved the theological differences between his Catholicism and the Mormons, and succeeded where others had been excluded. His accounts of these exchanges were entertaining. One day he wore a yellow tie, and none of the butchers would talk with him. He had not one order that day. Fortunately, someone told him this was considered as a sign of homosexuality, which was the most heinous derangement known to man. The Bible and Joseph Smith had so ordained.

Eventually the adventuresome life wore thin, and he wanted to settle in one place. He tried a regular sales route with Rath's, but this became boring. He then moved to California and worked for Montgomery Ward. His sales experience and smooth talking moved him along until he became a plumbing department manager. This is where he endured for thirty years. He was offered promotions, even as a store manager, but he refused. He never gave any indication that he knew why he did this. He had never heard of the Peter Principle, but it appeared to me that he was an ideal example. He retired when the company closed. Now he has coffee most mornings with a small group of old men, washes his car, reads the newspaper avidly and sits in the driveway watching the traffic. If he has regrets, they are probably less painful than are mine for him. Hopefully, he doesn't realize how different his accomplishments could have been if he had not been so negative and flippant, and had gone to college. His self image might have been so different. Possibly, he would have chosen better books to read while sitting in the driveway.

Chapter 15

Born Again

I am having an epiphany. It sounds like a religious experience, but it isn't really unpleasant, or a problem. In fact, it has been coming on for a long time and I just didn't realize what it was. Now that I know, I am quite comfortable with it. I am changing who I am. The new me is an Indian. The old one was almost one hundred percent German, and I liked kraut and beer and Strauss waltzes, but very simply, there are more benefits being an Indian. Ever since I was a boy I have liked Indians, although I don't know if I ever met one. In the movies they were interesting, but they mostly had bad parts, everyone except Tonto. That seems to be changing, although there aren't many western movies anymore, and there's lots of unemployment. It probably is because there are so many of us Indians now that there isn't the same novelty or excitement about us.

My conversion or rebirth shifted into high gear last month when I was talking to my brother on the phone. He lives in California, and they have some different ideas there; they call them progressive. Anyway, this whole thing is probably a little like having a sex change operation. You just know something isn't right, and it just keeps nagging at you until you wake up and face it. It was a surprise to me, but I think I've got it right now, and will grow into the idea of who the new me is. First I have to change my name. Most of the basket ball players have taken on fancy new names that make them sound more interesting, but that's just a put on. They aren't real Arabs. On the other hand, an Indian name is very different. It has to say something about the real you. I have always been an honest, direct simple person so the idea of being *Straight Arrow* seemed natural enough, but it sounds pretty ordinary and overused. As I was fumbling along with this I came up with the idea of *Gray Arrow*. I'm old enough that it is appropriate, and it gives me dignity. I can just see myself sitting in a tribal council, and everyone is listening respectfully to my wisdom.

The next thing I have to do is decide what tribe I belong to. I never thought about this when I was German. We had a lot of Goths in our background, but no one ever took that seriously. Today if you want to succeed as an Indian you have to get into the right tribe or you won't even have a casino, and then what would you do for a living? I read in the New Yorker magazine last month, when I was in the dentist's office, about a tribe in Connecticut that used to have only a few hundred members. Would you believe it? This idea is so popular now that there are about sixteen thousand who have proved that they have a few drops of Indian blood in them, and they are entitled to share in all the goodies. This idea has come a long way since my brothers were hunting buffalo and scalping white eyes. Incidentally, I don't know how you prove how many drops of a certain flavor blood you have.

All of that doesn't really bother me. I am just going to stand around on the street corner wearing my new black hat with a feather in it, and wait for someone to come by and adopt me. I hear they do that a lot to try to increase the voting membership of their tribe. I'll just wait for the best offer. Now getting back to my brother, where I really got the flash of light that put me onto all this. He was saying that his kids went through school free in California. When I asked him how this happened he said, "Because they were native Americans." So, I asked what does that mean. He said, "Well of course they're native, they were born here, and they never been anyplace else." Sometimes he says things that don't make sense, but this sounded reasonable. Why didn't I think of that. It must be that we don't think like folks in California. Anyway, that was the answer he gave to the people at school when the kids started in first grade, and the papers got marked that way, and all through the grades, and even into college, everyone seemed nice and happy to have them there because the government paid money to the school system for them. It helped that his wife was really born on the Rosebud reservation in South Dakota, where her folks were teachers for a Quaker outfit. What all of this leads to is that if my brother is the father of native American kids, I must be the uncle of native Americans, so obviously I have to be at least part native American. Isn't it surprising how one thing leads to another so logically? Now I'm looking for someone to teach me sign language, and a few grunts. All I can do so far is say, "How," and no one really understands that I'm working on becoming one rich Indian. Maybe I will eventually have to move to California where they understand about naturalized German Indians.

Chapter 16

The German Helix

In my musings I try to identify the source of my varied traits, which gene pool contributed what. I have a vivid picture of the Rubert's persona and way of life. I credit them with the colorful and emotional qualities I most value in myself, but the Kascht half of the equation is vague. I filter my memory for an outstanding event or an exciting happening. It is plodding and mostly unrewarding. Am I a haploid being, with only genes from one side expressed? I know it isn't that simple. I really spent much time with them, but even Christmas doesn't stand out. The family would go to midnight Mass and later we were all together, cousins, aunts and uncles, gathered around the spindly paper imitation tree, but I don't remember any special gift, or singing or sweet emotion or even nonsense. Then at noon we returned for dinner, but I don't have any image of the details. I am haunted by a glaring memory that children were supposed to be quiet at the table.

Grandma Kascht was my soup grammy. Stooped and withered, weighing little more than a hundred pounds, she was most comfortable in her rocker in the basement, peeling apples and vegetables. This was also the setting for her breathing treatments. She had severe asthma, and during coughing attacks she sat bent over a saucer of smoldering powder that gave off an unpleasant acrid smoke. It was extremely irritating, but that was its benefit. This induced a productive cough and somehow relaxed the asthmatic spasms. It was the only treatment available. She was resigned to this and never whimpered or complained. She gardened enthusiastically. This was the essence, growing and peeling, that best characterizes her. It resulted in a perpetual pot of soup simmering on the low heat back burner. Culinary excellence wasn't part of the process. She just provided nourishment three times a day. Occasionally she baked, but it was similarly routine and lacking drama. The dessert that we feared most was a bowl of cut up cubes of red Jello with milk poured over them.

Grandpa was a small man, thin and erect. If such a paradox is possible, he was a miniature Prussian Kaiser guard. In every way he was the opposite of Grandpa Frank. I don't recall ever having called him by name. Grandpa "Jacob" just didn't invite familiarity. He walked to work at seven in the morning and came home at five in the evening. I think he did some kind of machine work, but it was in a man's world, not subject for home discussion. He was quiet, stern, inconspicuous and absolutely no fun.

Four children survived this oppressive climate. The oldest, Agnes, was the *Head Cashier and Bookkeeper* at the Rath Meat Packing Company. This was a proud, often repeated identification. Every morning she spoke by phone with her counterparts in the financial world centered in Chicago, assuring that all things were in proper orbit. She was the ranking woman in the organization, and in 1932 she was paid a salary of $200.00 a month. This was eloquent testimony to her ability, years before anyone thought of an MBA. She was unmarried, and gave tender meaning to the usually unflattering term "maiden lady". She attended mass daily. Aunt Agnes loved me. She left a thousand dollars in her will for my education, but we lived two years on that as a more urgent need.

Next was John. He was humorless, at least that was my feeling. He had a nice dress-up job at a drug store. I didn't know what he did.

GOOD GENES, LUCK, LOTS OF PRAYERS

I always thought drug stores were places where you bought ice cream, but I couldn't imagine uncle John making a Sunday. It was a quiet family fact that he sold medicinal alcohol in the days of prohibition. This didn't seem to cause the family shame. Instead, Uncle John was popular, in demand, and quite successful. Eventually he opened his own drugstore, and even joined the country club. In spite of this success, he always charged me for penny candy; he even wanted to see the money first. After my father died, they were good to us, and sometimes invited us to Sunday dinner.

Number three used up all the quota of beauty and charm in the family. She was a perky, attractive brunette, capriciously named Viola. She married and had two children. Her husband died and she moved back home with her parents. Then she died of tuberculosis.

Next it was my father's turn. Lawrence was the youngest. I don't know much more about him and his ways than I do about the others in the family. He went to college at Creighton. How he got there, what moved or inspired him, I don't know. He must have been a challenge for the elders to understand, something of a maverick. As German parents, life was simple and orderly, an unreasoned succession of putting one foot ahead of the other, until one day you just stopped. Obviously, they had respect for education, but it could just as easily have been intimidating. Nonetheless, he made it. He was the last of the four to die. I was fourteen. In that time I had been to a dozen funerals, but never to a wedding. Grandma was the survivor, durable, resilient and wizened.

On paper, this appears to be an orderly progression of the family to mild success, without drama or warmth. It has none of the self-awareness of great tragedy. There were occasional elements of Thoreau's "the mass of men lead lives of quiet desperation" and even the relentless march of the quarry slaves in Thantatopsis, but it was not epic. This was grinding, plodding slightly upward, as little people inched toward their hope for a better eternity. Where do I fit in this continuum? Is my heritage the idealized free world of the farm, or is it the discipline of a pinched life doing what has to be done? Am I trapped in my Germanic Gemini genes? There is an unlikely answer: maybe Presbyterian guardian angels were watching over me.

Chapter 17

Idols to Ideals

Many of the warmest and brightest memories of youth are fueled by heroes. They influenced us more than preachy appeals to reason, affectionate cajoling, or even threats. They were a real and vivid presence, a pervading force that penetrated to the subliminal, and guided us in ways unrealized.

Heroes ranged from national figures like Lou Gehrig, Tom Mix or Lindberg, to a neighbor who could pick corn faster than anyone else around. Best of all, we could select those we wanted for our personal firmament. The available stock was endless, and we could easily replace those that waned, or when our interests changed.

Unfortunately, true heroes have gone out of style. They have been supplanted by megastars who court wealth and notoriety rather than excellence, and are not deserving of respect. However, our childish yearning remains unchanged. Within our deepest selves, pushed down and unfulfilled, is the continuing hunger for an idol. At a conscious level we may deny it, and parade our self-sufficiency. We are a society of sophisticated independents, but beneath the bravado, everyone needs a John Wayne.

In my life, religion has served well as a source of models and inspiration. It was not the negatives of the commandments, or the gloom of hell fire. Rather, it was the flavor and color of centuries of tradition, and the warmth and dignity of good people. In this light I page up images of those who taught me.

Nuns were the most distinctive logo of our special world. Occasionally someone would notice that we didn't eat meat on Friday, or that we had ashes on our forehead at the beginning of Lent, and they might conclude we were a bit different, but when they saw nuns they knew exactly what they were; they were *The Religious*. Even priests weren't as distinctive. They were lumped into the category of *Clergy* and were lost among all the other *Men of the Cloth*.

Nuns were at the same time specific and generic. They were stick figures, or more likely, blocks, usually of black, with few individual attributes. Their faces were framed by a white wimple that pinched tight, giving them rounded, slightly puffed cheeks. No wisp of hair ever escaped under the wimple, so we assumed they were either bald or shaved their scalps. A veil shrouded their head and flowed down to merge in continuous black with a straight hanging frock that erased every hint of body parts. With great solemnity this was called *The Habit*. As we grew older there was occasional renegade speculation about what the younger ones were hiding under it all.

Nuns came in two varieties: short and dumpy, or tall and commanding. The latter taught eighth grade and coached baseball. Most of them had men's names. It was explained to us that they were honoring their fathers by this living memorial, but we thought it just suited their personalities better. The little ones often had emotional names like Immaculata or Dolorita, or the name of a great saint. We never realized they also had last names, which of course they did, because they didn't write checks or sign papers.

From behind, they were anonymous. At first glance, the front pews of kneeling nuns appeared empty, but turned around, face to face, their individuality was surprising. They exerted themselves and compressed their entire being into their face. It was their only way to express what they really were. Some were bubbling, smiling and sparkling-eyed. Others were serene and reflective. A rare one was beautiful with a hint of mystery and shadow. These Ingrid Bergman types were our ideal of pristine perfection, before our sweet simplicity was tarnished by tiptoeing in the quicksand around the sixth commandment.

Those who really live in memory, standing out despite the softening of many years, were the large ones. They had firm faces that often surprised you with a grin, and large farmer type hands, usually holding a pointer or ruler, although this wasn't a necessary prop. They were of the real world, pragmatic, contrasting with the ethereal and spiritual types. Some images are still chilling. Sister Thomasita presided over my eighth grade. On opening day she alerted us that we were now ready to be treated as men. This wasn't very meaningful, but it sounded ominous, as her excuse for whatever happened in the next nine months.

One day when the catechism reading included the advice: "Turn the other cheek if a man strikes you," Homer Harper, the leader of the perpetual opposition, said, "When I hit 'em they can't turn the other cheek." With a predictable reflex, sister splintered the ruler on his knuckles, convincing him that he did not have a proper Christian view. She then took a yardstick from the closet, flexed it like a fencing master, and in quiet control, resumed a discussion of the beatitudes with a most attentive class.

The magic of "Captain, may I?" was only make believe, just a game. In sharp contrast, "Ster" was the password for survival. For those who don't speak Catholic, it translates into "Sister," and was elided to form "Yester" and "Noster" as the occasion required. It was prefixed to every sentence we spoke in class. No word in my vocabulary evokes more awesome memories.

I became a connoisseur of parochial education when I was young. My father said, half jokingly, that it was cheaper to move than pay rent, so I was exposed to a variety, mostly Benedictines,

Dominicans, and Notre Dames. These were uniformly robed in black, so I was startled to see a nun in brown standing before my sixth grade class at St. Mary's. She was my first Franciscan. The color was different, but the discipline and ambience were the same common denominators. She introduced herself. "I am Sister Mary Carmel." She raised her right hand, turned it sideways and extended the middle finger. Then with her left forefinger she pointed to the base of the extended finger and said, "See that bulge. That is muscle. It comes from slapping children." She smiled and we began class. In retrospect this is overly dramatic and even jarring, but in real time it simply was the way things were, and they worked. We were mostly happy. We studied, we schemed, we misbehaved, and we accepted punishment as being deserved, but secretly we knew it was worth it. Overall there was very little turmoil in class or on the playground. The Sisters' presence assured that there was only one acceptable scenario: total, non-violent, passive surrender. Most surprising to my adult recall, parents were not distressed or indignant, and did not intrude. These memories and values have been constants in my life, and the nuns were unyielding markers defining the slalom course we lived.

When I became a parent I wanted our children to have some of these experiences. The nuns were still there, although dressed more creatively. Teaching was their business, and they were still dedicated to it, but the times and tempo had changed, and so had I.

ℰᗡᏟᎡ

In the spirit of the sixties, with its tide of activism, I became involved in the operation of the schools, and even presumed to give my opinions on theory and methods of education. After all, I had graduated from a teacher's college. Also I had developed enough maturity and ego strength to say both syllables of "sis-ter", even occasionally with an imperious rising inflection.

Our second son was a free spirit, sometimes bordering on rascality. He purchased a *pagan baby* single-handedly to save its soul, using six dollars that properly belonged in his newspapers collections. We only learned of this after he proudly informed us that the class had voted to name their class baby after him. Further questioning about this surprising honor, produced much writhing and sweat, and eventually, the painful truth.

In the sixth grade, he also masterminded a mass book drop at a predetermined minute, sending the nun into near hysteria. Her name, Dolorita, was poetic and prophetic. The poor sister relayed her accusations to the superior and demanded justice and maybe retaliation. She had as evidence a note that had been passed through the class explaining the procedure, and setting the precise time when it would happen. Allegedly, this had been written by our Stephen. The maligned, innocent youth, exophthalmic and tearful, swore to me that he was not the perpetrator. I assumed my best parental manner, after the model TV father, Ward Cleaver, judiciously listened to both sides, then expressed total confidence in his truthfulness. This was so unexpected and apparently undeserved, it destroyed his defenses. He broke down, and confessed. Perhaps it helped him to find the courage to do it, when I offered to take the note to my friend, the Chief of police, and have the expert on handwriting analyze it to prove that it was not Steve's. Thereafter he regarded me with concern, perhaps too devious to be a father.

A short time after this, the nun withdrew from teaching. Rather than any causal relationship to this episode, we assumed it was simply some quirk or deficit in her personality, and undoubtedly, a contemplative order would suit her better.

GOOD GENES, LUCK, LOTS OF PRAYERS

Steve's next aberration was less dramatic, but had a better outcome. In eighth grade he was accused of having disrupted a class by standing outside the window and making faces. The accuser was a looming presence named Sister Aurelia. We didn't know the origin of her name; it was unlikely that it was from anyone in the family. Her bearing was more consistent with a Laker point guard than a Roman philosopher. Without any inquisition, or background exploration I asked Steve if he had done *It*. He said no, and I believed him instantly. He had been sensitized on the first fiasco, and was wary of me. I faced upward to her, five foot six against something nearing six feet. I had on my side the authority of being on the school board and chairman of the personnel committee. I gave her the full two syllable rising inflection treatment, and said in essence, he didn't do it, matter closed. Possibly this was a bit arbitrary, but blind trust paid off, and Steve and I have been best friends ever since. Today he is a parent, a teacher and a staunch disciplinarian.

In our daily life with the sisters we developed a symbiosis, something like sharing a foxhole. It was a comfortable arrangement, knowing, more or less, what was likely to happen next. The priests were not a natural part of this amiable cold war. They were also of the Catholic world, but they were remote, sometime visitors from another universe.

‽⍺

Through centuries, Mother Church had sampled the spectrum of humankind, from peasant to prince. They were ordained as priests, and endowed with sacramental equality. They came for the noblest of reasons, because God had called them, or from more mundane motives: political convenience or chicanery, a too crowded family or to comply with a mother's aspiration, or most ignoble, to escape personal inadequacy.

The pastor was nominally in charge of the school. He, or a curate, visited the classroom weekly, as a formality to assure orthodoxy and to bask in deference. He rarely spoke about anything other than the standardized catechism. Some tried to tell a joke to reassure us, but no one ever laughed. It was a pointless exercise that later in life reminded me of the inspections by visiting generals. Not knowing what they were looking for, they found nothing. Then, like grandparents, after going through the motions and stirring everything into a froth, they could go home to whatever else needed their attention.

We knew in our private minds that they were human, people like us. They weren't as type cast as the nuns, but there were broad categories. One first noticed they were either young or old. The old ones were pastors, either grumpy and authoritarian or round, jolly and likely alcoholic. The young ones were often very young. They were anxious about having been entrusted with mysteries they did not understand, nervous about the privileged confidences they knew, and self-conscious with their authority. The fortunate ones were those whose parents, at least a mother, were parishioners. This earned them special affection and tolerance, and the mothers forever after basked in reflected glory and respect. The newly ordained aura eventually wore thin, and life settled into a taxing routine of absolving sins and saving souls from damnation. As the years wore on, they merged and morphed into the mold of the pastor, and began to share his tribulations. On the few occasions when I passingly considered the priestly vocation, I was frightened by the image of loneliness.

We had a bit of an inside view. We almost had a priest in the family, but the launching was aborted. A cousin of my father was well along in his studies in the seminary, when he decided to leave. It was beyond reason, almost unheard of and scandalous. No one could guess "Why," and he chose not to say. Inasmuch as he never married, everyone happily concluded that he had not been seduced from his priestly commitment. He had a wonderful voice, and repaid the family's patience and trust by singing at all of their funerals.

My parents, and most of the parishioners, seemed ill at ease and fidgeted in the presence of the priest. A few people played cards or had a drink with them, and there were the appointed trustees who rubber stamped the things the pastor wanted done. Unfortunately, few people realized that this wasn't the way the priests wanted it. This was the distorted image created by an insecure laity, who needed a noble conduit to God. The priests lived out this misconceived fantasy of a separate nobility.

These recollections of priests are tempered by my exposure to the ministers of my Presbyterian grandparents. I went to church with them regularly, and was as comfortable with *"The Old Rugged Cross"* as with the *"Ave Maria."* I liked all the singing and the energetic oratory. In those days priests were not skilled speakers. They were catechists and labored the details of the commandments and church law, without much inspirational insight into human nature. They did find opportunities to intersperse appeals for money.

The little farm community church was something of a mission served by student ministers from the seminary in Dubuque, ninety miles away. It was a discouraging assignment. The pay must have been pitiful, but the student was assured of a full scale, show-off Sunday dinner. He also was likely to be subjected to the attentions of a hopeful nubile daughter. I watched a succession of these young men through the years. At first I judged them to be less perfect than our priests because they were permitted to marry, and seemed to be especially focused on it. This seemed like a major defect. I have revised my view of this with the passing years, and continue to share vicariously the loneliness I imagine in the lives of our priests, as they struggle for perfection.

Chapter 18

Ode to an Uncommon Man

My first view of him was from a carefully chosen back row seat near the door in Sophomore English. I was half trying to stay awake and in focus after a night's work at the meat packing plant. He strode to the front of the room in full professorial bloom and began his performance. Neither of us was much aware of or concerned about the other.

Up to that time much of my life had the sameness of cold oatmeal, gray and usually lumpy. Mother, young brother and I were authentic Horatio Alger, the proud poor, in the days before Welfare was invented. We worked and scrambled, drudging one foot in front of the other in a succession of empty days.

Without inspired resolve, I simply knew I was going somewhere, just to get away. College was the pathway. It wasn't well lighted and there were few markers. English 114 was required for graduation, so I was there.

At some point, after a few weeks, I realized that I looked forward to the class; I moved toward the front of the room and began to participate uncertainly in the discussion. The subject had changed from English to Ideas. A few of the students began to take form and said Hello. The professor was no longer anonymous. I learned that he was H. Willard God. This was no casual, clever nickname flipped off randomly over a beer, and it certainly wasn't derogatory. H. Willard Reninger was so respected, even revered, that the serious students of the IN group referred to him simply as God. Of course, this was in his absence. In time I was adopted by the group and also assumed the privilege.

At first I was a bit disappointed. He may have held his own as a Deity, but in the flesh he was very medium: mid-forties, average height, receding hairline, prominent nose, glasses and a pipe. Beyond this no one really catalogued him. It would have been presumptuous to inquire about the hat size of the Almighty. Anyway, we wouldn't have agreed on a detailed description. So much of him was our individual projections that each preferred his own image.

At the lectern he was transfigured. He had an unnerving manner. A quick glance at the page, then he looked up and recited three or four lines, while his eyes patrolled the class, snapping us to attention, and injecting insight into each mind that had blinked open. He was not just a reader, he was the author creating on the spot. His voice was the ideal instrument, flexible in range and volume, confidential and seductive, or thunderous and challenging. He had perfect pitch for ideas. His reading had more flavor and meaning than the author had put in. Print became breathing essence, not just words. We met and knew the authors.

I shared callouses hoeing with Henry David, had tea with Emerson who was too reserved for me, compared the common spirit of Frost's granite with Iowa loam, then escaped to the sensuous extremes of the literary Paul Bunyan, Thomas Wolfe.

At first we knew little about his life, nor did we care. Outside of class professors inhabit a vague intellectual outback. In time we developed a less formal, but still self-conscious, personal relationship. It is not easy to fraternize with God. The group met at his home in the evenings to read plays and poetry. We were joined by the local greats, farmer-poet James Hearst, who had been crippled in a diving accident, and Ruth Suckow, a popular prairie novelist.

We eventually matured enough to see Reninger, the man, and on at least one occasion in distress, when he was running low on fig newtons for the group. It was not surprising that his increasing humanity did not diminish him.

At one meeting Sandberg was to read his poetry and sing. He needed a guitar for accompaniment, so I was sent scurrying about campus to find one. When the great man of the People came to his songs, he patted the borrowed guitar and said in his rumbling paused accent, "Yes sir, I don't ever travel without Old Betsy." That moment one of my archangels stumbled.

Other visitors came to share what was beyond our cornfields, and under Reniniger's guidance we explored the firmament, and discovered the first star of the morning, Emerson. "Trust thyself. Every heart vibrates to that iron string." Surely this was noble language, but I didn't understand how it applied to my life. Men have been stirred by rousing oratory and grand writings to sail on, or to climb to unseen goals without ever learning the reasons. Sometimes the cadence is more than the content, and I marched to the rhythm of the words. The understanding came in later years when I appreciated the universality of Wisdom. "When we read the works of great men, we often find our own rejected thoughts returning to us with a certain alienated majesty."

Thoreau was next on the horizon. He was part of my world. I felt true kinship with him, an idealist, but a simple country man considered strange by his neighbors. I, too, had walked a field belonging to another, taking the beauty of the sunset, then going my way without the farmer knowing what he had lost. I also understood the deliberate impulse to go to the woods, to drive life into a corner, so that when I came to die I would not discover that I had not lived.

Reninger paraded endless ideas through my meager life, showing the rich diversity of man's imaginings. Some took hold, others were lost, ideas I was not yet ready to conceive. Of these many voices, the clearest was Robert Frost. No staid New Englander, he was flesh and bone to me. At times of greatest decision in my life I heard him twanging: "Two roads diverged in a yellow wood, and I, I took the one less traveled by."

Religion inevitably intrudes into the formation of a person. It may be inherited, almost gene-linked, so that it is beyond question, but anyone aspiring to intellectualism must deal with it, at least passingly. Reninger rarely spoke of religion. His willing disciples would have listened and eagerly spread his gospel, but he was after our minds, not our souls. He spoke comfortably and without bias when religious writings appeared in the curriculum, but he never revealed his own preference. As near as he came was bemused approval of the anecdote about Thoreau's deathbed scene when the minister asked, "Henry, have you made your peace with the Lord?" to which he reportedly answered, "I didn't know we had been quarreling." This natural, non-theologic position suited him.

I was born a Roman Catholic, and as such had little inclination to question. Some of my new-found intellectual friends thought this was inconsistent with an otherwise inquiring mind, and that I should do something about it. Accordingly, I enrolled in a course of independent study of comparative religions. I read reformers, revolutionaries, mystics and ascetics, Aquinas and lesser scholastics. I concluded that the most active minds in more than two thousand years did not offer anything with a more convincing claim to the Truth. My concluding masterwork was a pompous thesis entitled, "*The Development of the Logos,*" which I really didn't comprehend

In the words of Omar, "I went out by the selfsame door by which I entered," and remained Catholic. I liked the ritual and warmth, the color and tradition, and the security. I even partly understood the Latin. So, I decided to be peaceful and use my energies learning things that more readily lent themselves to exploration.

From Reninger's insight I adopted his version of the principles of Cardinal Newman's APOLOGIA, "That life is worth living is the most difficult of proofs, but the most necessary of assumptions. Posit something into being, then live as if it were true." This has kept me calm when thinking about eternity and other imponderables.

Inevitably I had to leave this sanctuary. With prompting from the Army I applied to Medical School. I listed Reninger as a reference. Years later I learned he had written:

"To whom it may concern: This is to recommend to you a young man who has an uncommon liking for good books."

I enjoy imagining the effect this tangential, cryptic note had on a committee of Philistines. Despite this I was accepted.

ဆဝ

Eventually our biocurves crossed. I visited from time to time and in later years I even called him Bill. He was delighted when I would recall a favorite line, and he would then expand what I had haltingly started.

The sepia of age has not softened the painful memory of him slouching strapped in a wheelchair, dried food on his bib, sharing a table in the nursing home with my mother. She with gun metal gray hair carefully coiffed, overly red lips earnestly talking with no one listening. Even in those last hollow days, he might announce that he was a teacher, then ask if I knew a certain author. He could still react to a quote, but mostly he was in a world apart. I prayed that it was brimming with grand ideas and peopled by his idols.

Sadly I watched them, my earthly mother and the father of my intellect, together a cameo of the seventh age of man, sans everything. Then he died, simply, as he would have described Thoreau's passing.

Among his students were many who became noted teachers and professors. The jewel of his legacy was a poet laureate, and there are those of us unrenowned whose minds were illumined and our lives enriched.

I knew him for more than forty years. He had launched a desolate boy into a world that he made vastly more wondrous and beautiful. As I went my destined way, he was there, and in quiet moments or in times of greatest trial his echo came through to guide and comfort me.

Our lives had diverged, but the sharing of core values, morality and the search for truth remained unchanged. Together we had taken "...the road less traveled by, and that has made all the difference."

Chapter 19

Em and M

I was probably ten years old when I first learned of Aunt Emily. She was remote and mythic, something like Santa Claus. Appropriately, she sent us a check at Christmas after my father became sick. Her name was always mentioned with excitement, and a hint of uncertain reverence, like she was too wonderful to be true, or maybe she would just disappear if we talked too much about her. I knew my folks were cautious. The most important thing to realize is she wasn't really my aunt. She wasn't even a blood relative. I couldn't understand the complicated linkage in those days, but she was the half sister of my real aunt, the one who had married my father's brother, uncle John. We would have liked for it to have been a closer tie, but it wasn't. We just had to pretend.

I didn't meet her until I was eleven or twelve. She had come all the way from Chicago to visit her sister, and she came to visit my dad. He had been the best man at his brother's wedding, and Emily was the bridesmaid, so they had shared happier days. She arrived in a Lincoln limousine with a chauffeur. There it was, parked in front of our dirty gray stucco duplex, four blocks from the meat packing plant. I imagined everyone for blocks around was peeking through the curtains. I felt so important it took a week for the shine to wear off my life. I remember seeing her get out of the car, wearing a mink coat, and the colored man holding the door for her. It was exactly the way they did it in the movies. Then she came into our house, sat on the lumpy sofa in our front room and smoked with a long cigarette holder. I don't think she noticed much about me, but that was alright. Fairy godmothers don't have to do much. It's enough that they are there. I had no problem adopting a rich aunt, and exaggerating a bit for my friends. The magic was magnified by her remoteness. She sent an occasional check for the next few years, and whenever aunt Anna talked about her, we knew who she was. Then we conjured our own special images of what she was doing. I didn't see her again until a year after my father died, when I was in high school.

The biggest thing on the list of claims to fame for our town was the Dairy Cattle Congress. We were sure that it was known throughout the entire United States. It was so important that the schools, even the high school, closed for one day to let the kids go. Inasmuch as we lived in the best farmland in the country, if not in the whole world, it didn't seem unusual that this would be the best farm and dairy show. Ordinarily, I would go with friends, and wander around, checking out everything from the girls to the special life-size sculpture of a cow made out of real Iowa butter. We walked through rows of barns, where the proud and nervous 4-H farm boys pampered and beautified their entries. The cows were curried with special brushes that gave a squiggly effect to the hair, much like the marcel wave that was then popular with the ladies. The cows were patted and kneaded like Kobe beef. We mirrored in the chocolate eyes of the Brown Swiss, and warmed to the sweet softness of the pink-tan of the Ayershires. We were skittish about being squashed by a misstep of a Percheron. We went through the routine exhibits of chickens and ducks, and got mildly excited about six-hundred-pound pigs that could scarcely get to the feeding trough, but we were sophisticated veterans of previous shows, and were in high school, so we had to go through the motions with proper boredom.

This special year was very different. I went with my mother, brother and aunt Anna and girl cousins I usually didn't bother with. We went into the riding horse barn. These were beautiful animals, shining coats, braided manes, and arched tails. They were tense and nervous, on display, and coquettishly seemed to know it. We came upon one box stall with a mounted placard identifying: *"Emily Genius."* This was it. Aunt Emily had shipped one of her horses to show and we had tickets. This was as big as things ever got in my early life. We had been invited to watch the dressage competition from her box. It was as magic as we could imagine. As the events in the hippodrome progressed, Emily reported to *Daddy* in the big city on the phone that had been installed at her seat. This was the ultimate luxury, even moreso than a chauffeur.

I did not see her again for about ten years, but she continued to send Christmas checks, and kept vaguely aware of us through her sister. I had a happy extra reminder of her when the movie, *"The Wizard of Oz,"* was shown, in 1939. One of the characters was Auntie Em in Kansas. Her role was unimpressive, but for me the name was enough. I worked this into my own talk whenever I could, even if it might not naturally fit the conversation. It made the real one just a little closer, and I could use all the magic and reassurance I could get. Even in later years, during the jelly and peanut butter days of our little family, I painted an exciting picture of my very own auntie Em. In our living room, on every rerun, the yellow brick road led off the TV screen across the carpet, and we anguished with the befuddled trio, heartless, witless and snivelling. We cringed under the malign cackling of the Wicked Witch, and prayed that goodness and right would prevail. Through it all, my Auntie Emily was an unseen force, always there as an ultimate refuge. I shared with our children, this mixture of my mind's magic, the way my Em was for me.

Years passed in monotony: family deaths, graduations, work and the army. With some surprise, I found myself in medical school.

I survived the rigors of the first two years and accepted the premise that I could actually do it. I was on the fringe of maturity and even began to feel some self esteem. Somehow, mother suggested that I call Emily. This wasn't the easiest or most natural thing to do, but she sent the address, and I called, probably from curiosity. I identified myself to the person who answered the phone, with a few words defining who and what I was. I didn't expect this to be especially meaningful. Emily took the call and sounded genuinely excited. She invited me to dinner the next weekend. My queasy confidence wasn't equal to this, but I knew there would never be the perfect time when I would be ready, so I said, "Yes."

The next Sunday afternoon I took the train to Winnetka, and then a taxi to the address, a very large white house. The door was opened by a poised black man, who didn't resemble Arthur Treacher or Jeeves. He seemed normal, and I marked him as a future friend and ally. My commanding knowledge of movie high society prepared me to be announced with a flourish of trumpets.

Instead, he quietly led me in and said, "Madam, this is your nephew, Robert."

Emily really hugged me and said, "My gosh, Bob, I wouldn't have recognized you. Come along and meet the others."

From then on, it was something like an ordinary party, just raised to the third power. There were eight or ten people. The women were elegantly dressed, but only two of the men were formal. There was one younger woman, a niece of someone, probably to counterbalance me, although it didn't seem like a very comfortable fit. She was attractive, but too polished, too upscale for me, Later I heard it said, in properly lowered voice, that she occasionally used dope. We continued around the room, without mishap, but the names and faces ran together, and I hoped I wouldn't be tested.

Then I met *Daddy* for the first time. His appearance suggested he had studied to fit the stereotype. He was about sixty, plump and pink, balding, and had soft hands. He smiled and crinkled. His voice was soft and pleasant, not that of a booming tycoon. He was a gentle man who could afford to be simple. I learned more about him in the next months, but we didn't become well acquainted, because he died a year later. He was typecast, the younger son in a prominent family. What should he do? The older brother was the president of the family business, and was very active in civic affairs, and a poster boy for worthy events. Daddy was content to do whatever he was supposed to, and enjoyed the good life. He was quite ordinary in that circle, nothing adventuresome, no notorious indulgences. I was most impressed by two insignificant things. He had attended a military academy with Edgar Rice Burroughs, the future creator of the legend of Tarzan. The other memorable distinction was that he took the train daily into town, as did thousands of others, but he owned an upholstered armchair in the club car. I could visualize him sitting there with a few of the equally select, enjoying coffee and a cigar, readying themselves to run the world for another day.

The most unorthodox thing he ever did was marry Emily. She was a young nurse at Passavant Hospital, one of the healing centers favored by the elite. How she got there is beyond my information. I never thought to ask. It was certainly as great a leap for a small town girl, as was my hegira. This was probably a subliminal denominator in our relationship, but I doubt if she ever thought about it. She was just too spontaneous to look for subtle causes. Possibly it was the quality of her back rubs that won him, but these were supported by a spirited and determined personality that contrasted sharply with the blasé, acute boredom of his usual associates. Looking like Lauren Bacall also may have helped. She must have encountered resistance and raised eyebrows from the matriarch of the family. Nonetheless, she was installed in a mansion in this northshore suburb, in charge of an established household. It consisted of a cook, houseman or butler, chauffeur, laundress and cleaning lady, and a personal maid. Emily quickly learned to refer to this assortment as a *ménage*. Daddy, who provided all this, seemed almost incidental. How she acquired the skills and poise for this role was a mystery we never discussed. She must have watched and listened intently, and she survived. As I saw her that evening she was comfortable and unshakable, as if she were prepared from birth for grandeur and command. In her words it was *panache*, but through the years she remained always an unpretentious aunt.

Dinner was announced. We entered the dining room, and it looked very much like in the movies. My mother had been most insistent about table manners, and I felt confident. I even remembered a little booklet on etiquette that had been distributed before our high school senior banquet. Suddenly I was jarred by seeing three forks. My past limit was two, but I applied the principle of working from the outside. The question was what to use them for. The first real hurdle was getting seated. Did I seat the lady to my right or left? This solved itself when one remained standing, so I assumed she was for me. I sat quietly, hands in lap. Everyone else leaned, reached and gestured. So much for book learning. We had soup, nicely identified by Emily as: *Crème de Poulet, à la Reine.*

I thought it referred to the river. I didn't say anything except that it was delicious. Some time, weeks later, I learned that *reine* means queen. Possibly, some of the others didn't know this. I was careful to spoon away from myself and not to slurp. At one point I encouraged myself by recalling that President Roosevelt used to crush crackers into his soup, even at State dinners, to put people at ease, but then what did he know about gracious manners? He was a Democrat.

There was a magic button hidden under the carpet at the hostess' chair, by which she signaled to the kitchen for service. The main course arrived, presented most formally by white gloved hands. This was panic time. Concerns about seating and silverware were minor. This was big time trouble. The main course was lamb. Iowa farm boys didn't eat lamb; certainly I never had. How did I know it was lamb? I paraphrase Gertrude Stein: a lamb is a lamb is a lamb. It tasted exactly as I knew it would, terrible. This was the ultimate test of my composure. I interspersed distracting conversation with tedious slicing, and carefully hid the minced bits under the peas. I forced an occasional bite which was washed down without a chew, and untasted. The world continued to turn, and eventually the meal ended. Our efforts at conversation wore out, and we left.

Emily was still an unknown, but we had made contact, and at least we would recognize each other. A few weeks later she again invited me to join her at dinner, this time at a private club in town, where we were admitted by showing our member's gold key. We were one on one. It was a reunion of simple Iowa farm folk. We rushed to talk, heedless of "*Robert's Rules of Order*" interrupting each other, ranging from how I got to medical school, to a description of the fancy victorian outhouse she had built for the hometown church. I was amused by occasional speech mannerisms, whether affectations or a carry over from early life, that must have caused the society mavens to raise an eyebrow and comment, "How charming." Maybe some even copied her. Instead of "Anyhow," she said, "Anywho." It wasn't a big thing, but it was distinctive. When a lovely lady says something like that while smoking with a six inch ebony cigarette holder, you know that Webster wasn't perfect. At dinner I was introduced to cold potato soup, and she cautioned me to pronounce the final "s" in Vichyssoise, because "It really isn't French, you know," I wondered who had taught her that. The greatest memory of the evening was Emily liked me. That was an unfamiliar awareness for me. I almost felt lovable. Even without money this aunt would be a keeper.

This relationship continued irregularly, on impulse, over the next two years until I graduated and left. During this time, Daddy died and she moved from the suburbs to a town house. This was a beautifully restored old row house, or brownstone, narrow and long, three stories, with fourteen foot ceilings. She furnished it with her treasures from the big house, oriental rugs, Aubussons, Gobelins, screens, silver, leather furniture and French colonial pieces, an eclectic motif. This was much more convenient so I visited often, and felt I was a part of the household. Em had retained her cook, former butler Roger, now converted to houseboy and chauffeur in this less pretentious setting, and a maid who also did laundry. The car was downsized, but fun. It was a Lincoln Zephyr, which was on the cutting edge of the new streamline design. This was a warm and happy interactive family, everything I had never known. I was well beyond the formative years, and had a substantial base of general knowledge and literature, but the refining of my tastes and appreciation of the good life date from these years.

I learned to tolerate and even like Scotch whiskey. She drank Oldfield's Blue Label. I therefore assumed it was the best, but I have never seen it since. I drank Chartreuse, which incidentally, she pronounced: "Chartrace," an affectation that pleased her, imparting a little extra French spin. I imagined the ripple effect of these innovations when other matrons tried to adopt them as something special. This was a startling liquor, yellow or dramatic green, with a spicy sinus clearing essence. Em said it was a distillate of the Cairo camel markets. I had been cooking for my mother and brother since age twelve, so I was especially impressed by Charlie. He was a jolly black man, totally in control of his kitchen. He occasionally announced that he had been the personal chef of General Black Jack Pershing. No one challenged this, and it made no difference. He was excellent. He lived before anyone was driven to the nouveau cuisine by concerns about cholesterol, or weight watchers. He was surprisingly creative, but he didn't aim at making a cover picture for Gourmet Magazine. He just wanted it to taste good, and it always did.

This was the essence of midwest plain cooking. My favorite part was the dressing he made for turkey. All that I had known was homogenized and gluey, tasting strongly of sage and onion. I didn't object because this was the standard preparation of my mother and grandmothers, and no one knew anything different. Charley's recipe was a medley of toasted buttered bread cubes, coarsely chopped onions and celery, nuts, raisins, apples, water chestnuts, chopped bacon and crumbled sausage, tarragon and sprinklings of chicken broth and dry white wine. The texture remained particulate and discrete, and the flavors married, but were still individually detectable. This has become a cherished standard, passed through our family. It makes for a very happy turkey.

Emily took me to the Wednesday matinee concerts of the Chicago symphony. This was unfair competition for medical school lectures. I mingled as if I really belonged with the chauffeured and mink set, and became glib about the performers like Horowitz, Marian Anderson and Heifetz. Em gave me her husband's monogrammed handkerchiefs, his silk ties with labels from France, Charvet et fils, his pipes, and she identified with special pride the Sassinis she had bought for him in Italy. She gave me his Leica, the first one I had ever touched. Her generosity was unlimited, and if I had believed this was the real world. I would have been ruined. Fortunately, this was a closed end relationship. I had to graduate and move on to an internship.

During this vulnerable stage of her life, she had reduced her social activity. The schedule was standardized, routine dinners with the same established friends and family. She had little contact with new people. Outsiders were not readily welcomed by the wealthy.

They lived a self-sufficient, almost cloistered life. Despite this, one man made it through the barriers. He owned a small hospital supply company, dealing in durable goods, mostly bedding and bath supplies. He especially targeted the Catholic hospital circuit. He was German, and spoke with a carefully cultivated accent that must have charmed the helpless nuns. He was in his late fifties, and reportedly had been a surgeon with the U.S. army in North Africa until he was disabled by a heart attack. He presented himself as a count and privileged to use "von" in his name or title. However, he preferred to be an unpretentious American citizen, named Adolph, and he asked to be called Dolph. I welcomed the opportunity to talk medicine with someone so widely experienced, but he patronizingly informed me that there was such a vast difference in our years and knowledge, I wouldn't understand him. His most frequent response was, "Just perfect your technique and everything will take care of itself." I never understood what that meant, but it discouraged further conversation. He smoked incessantly, holding his cigarette affectedly between thumb and forefinger; often, with his other hand he would take a nitroglycerine tablet for angina.

He lived someplace near New York city, and drove regularly to Chicago, stopping at the Catholic hospitals along the way. He stayed at Emily's while he was in Chicago. I suspected she had invested in his company. I met him occasionally; it was always a strained encounter. He varied from courtly to arrogant, depending on what he wanted to accomplish. Despite my reservations about him, he did contribute to my developing savoir faire. He used an after shave lotion known as Kolnwasser or 4711. He informed me this was the original scent developed in the middle ages to mask unwashed body odors. Certainly, no advertising campaign highlighted this indelicate fact, but I liked it, and bought it whenever I could.

The war ended and I was discharged in 1946. I bought my first suit in five years. It was such an occasion that I went to a so-called custom tailor. However, it was mostly a mechanized process; I was photographed from a number of angles against a calibrated grid, and the measurements were determined from them. I had one fitting session for minor adjustments. The suit cost sixty dollars. When I wore it for Emily to see, she approved of it, and of my appearance as a civilian. Contrarily, Dolph thought it was a poor fit, and he added another unasked opinion. The buttonholes on the sleeve plackets were only stitched, not actually cut. One could not unbutton and open them.

I was annoyed, and challenged him with a question, "How many would ever notice or care?"

His answer gave me new insight into the mind of a snob. "Not many, but those are the ones who count."

I was deflated. Emily had bought suits for him at her husband's tailor at a cost of four or five hundred dollars. I could appreciate there might be some difference. She called the tailor, with her usual generosity, and arranged for him to alter my suit, undoubtedly for more than its original cost. It probably fit better, but I didn't regain my pride and excitement.

At the time of discharge, I had been in the army for almost four years, three of them continuously in medical school. There was one quarter remaining before graduation. I was always sensitive and defensive about not having been in the actual shooting war, but I went where I was sent, and in a special way it had been demanding and tiring. I decided I would benefit from a vacation. I needed a change, exercise and a chance to make some money. Through a classmate who lived in Spokane, I found a job in a sawmill. Emily and Dolph jumped at this news, and thought it would be an exciting opportunity for a trip. I was the designated chaperone. We drove the Lincoln to Montana and on to Washington. The scenery was glorious. The atmosphere was overly teutonic.

After a few weeks of work, I returned to school, and then to my internship, ending this idyllic phase of my life with Em. A few months later she called to tell me she had heard troubling rumors about Dolph. She flew to his home in a small town on the Hudson, and unannounced, went to his address. As she reported it, he was living in a poorly maintained old house; he was scruffy and unkempt and he had a very real wife. This was the end of the deception and the romance, and certainly the tailored suits and financial support. There had never been a count "von" whoever, or even a doctor. This was simply the death of a salesman.

Emily returned to the security of her household and familiar circle, but she had an affinity for wealthy men, and soon she discovered, or was discovered by *Uncle Charlie.* He was a very reasonable replacement for Daddy Number One. He was from the East, and had an accent from Damon Runyan. It was more authentic than ersatz German. He was a large man, tall but not heavy, who had a natural rumpled appearance in spite of being carefully dressed. He boasted of wearing Diamond Jim Brady's garters. In relaxed moments he resembled a Bassett hound, with a gentle, pathetic aura. He got along easily with people in a typical Irish way. We didn't know much about him, but after the experience with Dolph, he received careful scrutiny, and a background check certified he was real and had substantial resources. These included large portions of Central Park West real estate.

Emily married him and moved to New York. I visited them at their home on Long Island when I was a resident in a New York city hospital, but I had little opportunity to know uncle Charlie. I returned to Milwaukee, and was teaching at Marquette University when I learned he had died. Emily returned to Chicago where she was at home. She moved into a suite at the Ambassador West, where she lived for years. In all those years I never visited her again, because she didn't invite me. She became withdrawn, but she called me regularly. My secretaries recognized her voice and dutifully got me out of whatever unimportant thing I might be doing. She then moved to a nursing home, which she generously endowed in exchange for remodeling two apartments, one for herself and one for her maid and companion. We continued our relationship by phone, but never in person, although we were less than a hundred miles apart. Time continued to tick. We both grew older, but she had a considerable head start.

One day I received a call from a downtown Chicago hospital, informing me that she was in the Intensive Care unit. My wife and I drove to see her. Mary knew of her through my years of description, but they had never met. When we saw her she was on a respirator, with all the life supports medical technology could provide. She had a tracheostomy, and could not speak. She recognized me, but was too weak to respond beyond a blink. I was distressed that I had neglected her, but I rationalized it was her choice, never to have invited me. I attributed it to her terrible pride. Years earlier she had broken a hip, which healed with a shortened leg, She wore a built up shoe and limped. She no longer was the commanding presence, that used up all the oxygen when she entered a room. She wanted me to remember her as she had been.

She remained vegetatively alive for almost a year. She died, and as she had directed, her body was given to a medical school. This was most difficult for me. There was no vapor trail, no final resting place, no way to visit her, no memorial. She was gone, almost as if she had never been, except for the larger than life memories I cherished of my composite aunts, Auntie Em and Aunt Mame.

Chapter 20

The Manufacturing Process

Being a doctor is something like being married. You receive a certificate that says you are. This starting point deserves a large, "So what." The real challenge is what you do with either of them. A much more meaningful sidelight is how you came to be in either of these situations. This far outweighs the arrival end point. What you brought with you largely determined the quality of the product. Many times my mother assured anyone listening that Bob was going to be a doctor. I am sure that the financial success and the esteem that goes with the title had much to do with her prediction, although today she would have done better with a finance major CEO. However, I probably was subliminally influenced more than I realized. I tacitly conceded that I would eventually enter Medical School, and I willingly registered as a Pre-Med so I could ramble freely through the curriculum without the limitations of a Major. I leisurely wandered a course that favored arts over science, thinking over memorizing. I may have lacked the esoteric details of embryology and advanced physical chemistry, but I had instead explored the beauty of French Drama from Racine to Moliere. I also ingested a rich dose of poetry and I could argue quite convincingly about comparative religions. I had acquired broad knowledge and refined appreciations, but by the admission standards of that time, I was less than ideally prepared factually to begin the study of medicine.

My personal inclination would have been to dally longer with the subjects that interested me. This was not to be. For good or bad, the Army had determined that we were involved in a war that threatened to be a long conflict, and the supply of doctors was insufficient. Consequently, the Army established its own program to manufacture physicians, utilizing existing medical schools. I was strongly urged to apply for this. I realized that the alternative was a second lieutenant commission in the infantry, so I complied, and was sent to Northwestern University Medical School. This was surprisingly generous and rational treatment, following the pronouncements of General Hershey, director of the draft, that what the Army most needed was men whose civilian occupation was killing people. Few recruits admitted to this.

Arriving at school from the army gave me a feeling of being different. My classmates, new college graduates, had a scrubbed puppy quality. Resentfully aware that I was a bumpkin from a small school, I walked heavily with a proverbial chip on my shoulder. Despite this, by some quirk, I was invited to join a professional fraternity. It seemed the simplest solution to my housing problem, so I did. Life was a drudging blur. Four academic years were jammed into three continuous calendar years. The academic phase of medical school was much like the popular perception. It was difficult and tiring, with long hours of study. It was mostly routine and undramatic, a process that had proved to yield a uniform product, very much like a sausage stuffer. After a couple of years of mechanical drudgery we began to appreciate that we were involved with something more than just rote learning. Increasingly we were concerned with the fragility of human mortality. We had to deal with the problems of society, poor living conditions, inadequate nutrition, despair and the bankruptcy of man's spirit. From observation and association with the men who were our teachers and icons, we slowly underwent an unseen transformation, and without preaching, acquired an increased awareness of the spectrum of the problems of mankind. We developed, with individual variation, the capacity for expressing unashamed compassion. We were on our way to becoming doctors, and ongoingly the real world corrected excesses of theory and technology, and kept us oriented to the essentials of life.

Chapter 21

Puck

It was worse than any Friday the thirteenth I could remember, and it was only Wednesday. This was as if predestined; from hour to hour a new problem popped up.

I overslept because my roommate, who sets the alarm, stayed at the hospital overnight. At rollcall the sergeant yelled at me for not saluting, and scheduled me for phone answering duty on Saturday. This was the only punishment he could order that was anything like peeling potatoes on K.P. in the real Army. Next, I didn't know the right answers when the prima donna chief of Surgery was grilling me. That's the way it went all through the day, right up to supper time. Then I made a dumb choice in the cafeteria. The meatballs were rubbery and the gravy was gray.

Finally, I thought things were under control. I got to my room on schedule. It was six fifteen. On the way up the elevator I had decided to have a half hour prophylactic nap, and then study. This was one of my very few free luxury options . The alternative was to study first until nine thirty, and then do a power snooze until ten, before the finishing blast. Tonight the room was more annoying than usual. It was a cubicle, just too small for two people. A well seasoned mediaeval monk might have been comfortable, but one of the new variety like Thomas Merton, would have started reading the classified ads. The view of the lake was the same one that cost fancy dollars at the Drake, but I usually forgot to look. This jumbled life was the result of being caught up in a hybrid scheme that the Army had devised, training its own doctors for a long war. These minor aggravations did remind me I wasn't being shot at on the beach at Anzio or Normandy.

I flopped on the bed, and as if I had activated it, the phone rang. Every fiber was in denial. Even my higher moral sense of obligation said, "Don't answer," but after six rings I did.

"Is Bob there?"

"Who's this?"

"Brent Marvitz from college, remember?"

"That was four years ago, but of course I remember you. What are you doing?"

"I'm in Chicago. Your mother gave me your phone number last time I was home. How about getting together for a beer tonight?"

"Brent, that's impossible. I have to study."

"I'm leaving in the morning." This kind of extra pressure just fitted the day. Inevitably, I agreed, just for an hour.

Ten minutes later and eleven floors down, I was sucked through the revolving door into rush hour. The wind that named Chicago swirled off the lake, snarling through icy teeth, and clawed to the bone. I turned up the collar of my army horseblanket coat, and head down, bobbed along on the crest of the snow-filled gusts. Brent had said, "714 North Clark Street." With all the fancy places on Rush street why would he pick that. Five minutes after I left Abbott Hall I wished I was studying. I passed the Chez Paree. The white sidewall limos were already lined up dropping off the big money for the Lena Horne show. They looked like caricatures out of Damon Runyon. I pushed on. There was Andre's bar where I spent many Saturday nights. Andre used us in his bantering challenge to the expensive clientele, "You certainly aren't going to let this lonely soldier buy his own drink." I was sacrificed for his gain.

Despite the weather and my confused schedule, I really wanted to see Brent. Nostalgia took over, and the night and the cold faded.

Brent was the one person in our self-anointed clique of literati that we expected to be famous. He was an anomaly. Whatever bearing it had on his persona, Brent had been a state champion high school wrestler in the 117 weight class, and in college he became a gymnast. The consequence of these was the graceful fluidity we envied. It wasn't deliberate or showy, and any attempt to describe it ended up in just words. Someone compared him to a human slinky. We thought our elite group was the next thing to the lost generation on the west bank in post-war Paris. We met randomly at a Lit professor's home to read poems, and solve the problems of philosophy in a misguided world. We stumbled into plays. Although the college had a respectable Drama department, none of us, except Brent, had ever had a part. He had once filled in a two line walk-on part, and was forever committed.

His repertoire grew, and soon he was reciting Shakespeare. Brent was diminutive, and actually quite odd looking. He had prominent frontal bosses that made him look very cerebral, maybe from another planet. He wore thick, wire-rimmed glasses. He was not leading man material, but his voice was so distinctive, mellow, inflected and interpretive that we could have listened to him reading a phone book. In the course of our excursions we tackled *A Midsummer Night's Dream*. Brent was cast as Puck, and Puck he became forever in the minds of our group. He was such a natural that he was sought by ladies clubs and various local affairs to give Puck readings. This publicity eventually grew into an expectation that he would become a professional actor, but I think much of Puck was a fabrication, an idealized image we projected. This was the time when our paths diverged. I went into the army. He did not because of poor vision. I had not heard of him or his doings until the phone call.

ဆဝ၇

Across Michigan and then State street to Clark; there it was,714, a generic "Bar and Grill." The lettering, once proud gold leaf, was now irregular, worn and crackled. The glass was permagrime cloudy. It was one of hundreds. The designation *grill* was a political coup. After the repeal of prohibition, every liquor license had to serve food. This recalled the wholesome nostalgic image of the good old days of the nineties, nickel beer and a free counter lunch. This also assured that it would come under the control of the Health Department, and be subject to inspection. Of course, this established the authority to close the bar for non-compliance, or maybe just whim. Food was available, but only an out-of-towner would think of eating it, but new leverage had been added to the booming protection industry. I walked in, uncertain if I would recognize Brent. This was obviously the cutting edge crowd, the cusp between upper blue collar and marginal white collar. It was the one-for-the-road wannabees. The patrons looked worn, tired of the day and of their lives. They lacked the energy and sparkle to look for a pickup. It was almost seven o'clock, and the regulars were thinning out. In one corner I saw Brent. He looked like I remembered, but he was obviously out of place. Probably for the same reason he recognized me. We hugged heartily. He looked slightly older, and his hairline had moved more than I would have expected in just four years. He was at a table, with three people seated. There were no introductions. For about the next fifteen minutes the world was just Brent and me. We filled in all the details of the time since graduation. My life had been simple, linear and traditional, but I didn't really get a clear picture of what Brent was all about.

Every five or ten minutes someone would stop at the table, Brent would jump up, grab his pork pie hat, bow exaggeratedly, and shake hands. The first time he did it, I laughed. It was like a vaudeville act. The second and third times, it was absurd, and confusing. A few people sat down at the table, but most just went through the routine and walked away. Those sitting at the table said very little. Mostly they seemed isolated and stared. One girl, or woman, whom he had called Marla was perched rigidly on the edge of her chair. I had the feeling that in her self-image she was cool and poised. It was an advertising shot of hauteur, but she looked pained as if every corpuscle was resisting the spinsterhood her angular body had decreed.

After about a half hour, she burst into a moan. "Oh Lord, it is so beautiful, all those waving fields of grain."

No one said anything. After a few minutes, one of the other women said, "I'm going to the john. Do you want to go, Marla?"

The answer from some way off place, "No, I have a remarkable condition known as a doubly distensible bladder. I rarely go. I correspond with others who have this. Just last week I received a letter from the Congo, written on a flat rock, and it described my condition almost exactly."

This was the point for me to leave. I didn't understand the group, and Brent had used up his interest in the good old days. I got up to go, but Brent blocked my way.

"You can't leave now. We have to do some business." He was holding onto my coat. I really hadn't thought about how strong he was.

"What do you mean?" I asked.

"What do you think all this was about? Just a stunt? I make a trip to Mexico every month and come back with a load of marijuana. I put three dozen cigarettes in my hat band every night and peddle them in bars like this. This is peanuts, but I want to move up. You can be part of it. When you're in the hospitals watch how they lock the narcotic case, where they keep the key. If you get morphine or demerol, I can move it. We'll split big money."

I tore away and ran to the door. "You're crazy. Either the law or the regular dealers will get you. This isn't a game that welcomes competition." The storm was forgotten. I ran all the way back to Abbott Hall. I couldn't study and I couldn't sleep.

I had a horror movie sense that I had stumbled into something that was major crime to an Iowa farm boy. People who got in the way of the mob didn't last long. For sure, even this minor narcotic traffic would be noticed by someone who could eliminate us with no more trouble than popping a pimple. Brent didn't seem to have the same take on it. Every day, every night, I expected him to call, either cajoling or threatening me. I assumed he had gone to Mexico, and should be back by now. He was ready for a new phase of his career, and I was a major obstacle. If I didn't go along with his idea, he could give my name to one of the street enforcers for the Big guys just to buy a favorable contact. Maybe he wouldn't do that, but it was one of the possibilities nagging deep in my mind. I even made two trips to the bar. I went on the same night, Wednesday. Brent wasn't there. I didn't recognize anyone who had been there with him, and I sure didn't ask any questions. After three weeks without any calls, I knew. I was as certain as I could be without actual proof, that Brent was no more. I visualized the rubbish and debris in the cluttered alleys I had seen on the home obstetric service. A body could be hidden forever in this jetsam, or in the thousands of public forest acres, a body covered by a few random leaves would just add to the mulch. In sorrowing memoriam I went to a park and read aloud Puck's epilogue from a library book I borrowed:

> *If we shadows have offended, Think but this, and all is mended,*
> *that you have but slumbered here while these visions did appear.*
> *And this weak and idle theme no more yielding, but a dream.*

Only the wind listened.

Chapter 22

Home Delivery

Like a special magnet, the lake had attracted living things since the time of the glaciers. It sustained a complex biome, and was a natural avenue for easy movement of the voyageurs. By mischance it lay in the path of westward migration, and was just enough of an impediment that many weary travelers slumped along its shores, and moved no farther. Clusters of same-colored or like-minded people were strewn along the lake, as randomly as pollen in a playful wind. Occasionally, it was understandable why one group or another was where it was, a mutual selection or fit, where the land best met the needs of the people, or where the types of people best tolerated each other's ways. However, one of the more puzzling developments, beyond simple logic, was a migration in the late 1940's, of southern blacks who espoused Islam, long before the broader community had even heard the word. Quite apart from any theology, it obviously was a status move, that set them distinctly above their neighbors. For their new promised land they chose an area ten blocks west of the Drake hotel, which in those days was the mecca of the elite and the elegant.

Here the lake splashed the gold coast, and provided a glittering backdrop for high rise apartments, opulent penthouses, gourmet restaurants and world renowned boutiques.

There were also more utilitarian inhabitants, high priced business addresses, and a prominent medical complex. This was not the broad shouldered, brawling hog butcher for the world, and the fog did not creep on little cat's feet; it slithered on mink. The resident Brahmins did not suspect, nor would they care, that there were different worlds just beyond their view, places one should not enter without a guarantee of safe passage.

ℬℭ

In another part of the Great City, at the crossing of Maxwell and Halstead streets, is a well known institution, the Chicago Maternity Center. As the name suggests, it provides for mothers-to-be. It is a clinic for prenatal care, and a clearing house through which a stream of medical students and residents pass on their way to deliver babies. Its unique distinction is the promotion of home deliveries, reversing the trend of going to the hospital. It has achieved renown for its low infant mortality, and has made a compelling case for delivery at home. This building is in the Jewish pushcart market area, which is popular with the more adventurous tourists, as well as the native Chicagoans in search of bargains. Those familiar with the culture flock to the market at first light to take advantage of the Jewish superstition that a merchant must sell to his first customer of the day, or risk disaster. This is a decided bargaining leverage, since, short of violence, the potential buyer could not be allowed to leave without making a purchase, even God forbid, if the owner loses money.

After the first rush, the bargain hunters and the tourists leave. The streets belong to the natives. Empty men sit on steps or in doorways, lean against the walls, pass a bottle partially hidden in a paper bag back and forth, alternating with a large deli pickle, having breakfast. No one moves with a sense of direction or purpose. Life is noisy, dirty and smelly. There is only survival.

GOOD GENES, LUCK, LOTS OF PRAYERS

Into this setting the young doctors come to do the good work of the center. They are from the medical schools in the city, and also from a few neighboring states. They are not prepared for the hazards. The Center experience is legendary, and a frightening lore has built up. Senior students who have survived, dutifully add to it year after year, and wave the specter repeatedly before the underclassmen. The students from the Chicago schools feel somewhat more confidant because they know the geography. This assumed advantage fades on the first encounter with the reality. For the fresh faced country boys, the experience is occasionally life threatening. A student from Wisconsin arrived on the street car, pushed through the crowds looking for the dormitory and suddenly lost his luggage in a brief jostling encounter. Instinctively he followed the man running into an alley. Predictably, the man turned and slashed his face and neck with a razor. It was not fatal, but this, and many similar incidents, nourished the menacing aura of the Center, so no one wanted to go there, but it remained a mandatory requirement for graduation.

℘)℃℞

Bob lay on the rumpled dormitory cot, unable to sleep. He was next in rotation for a delivery. Patients who had enrolled at the clinic for prenatal care would call when labor began, and a student would be dispatched to assist with the delivery. For some cases, if the prenatal record indicated possible complications, an intern would accompany the student. Bob was a senior at Northwestern, and was in the second week at the center. Time was passing and he was surviving, adjusting to the unseen threats and the simple problems of the area, lack of places to eat, and boredom. He tried to read. He tried to sleep. Finally the call came. It was ten AM. This was an all too common type of call. The woman was not registered and had not been seen in the prenatal clinic. She knew the routine from previous pregnancies, and simply called when labor began. This was always difficult; an unknown case, without background information, and usually with a problem.

An intern was sent with the student to assess the situation, from the vantage of one more year of experience. Usually, the students rode the streetcars, carrying the standard black doctor bag and wearing stethoscopes prominently around their necks, for instant identification, a talisman that could pass them to their destination. They counted on respect from the faceless people along the dark streets, whose indebtedness for past services might even include their own delivery by a student doctor. On this assignment the intern drove his car to North Edgewood, one of the ghettos in the shadow of the Gold Coast. They located the address, a basement apartment, and were met by a small man, bent and wrinkled beyond the estimated age of forty. "Yo is doctors? Ah is John Smith-bey. Mah wife is in heah."

Bob was surprised by the name, and asked for the spelling so he could properly enter it on the record sheet. There had been a brief discussion at the center about the new varieties of names and titles that had sprouted with the arrival of Muslims. It was Bob's first encounter. The husband certainly didn't appear different from the usual black. The spelling of the name, with the suffix *-bey* was different, and it had been explained that these newcomers thought this was an Arabic title indicating nobility. Bob soon learned that most names were exotic; some sounded like the Old Testament. Others were from the movies.

They entered a small room, sparsely furnished, with milk bottle cases turned on end as stools, an overstuffed sofa with holes in the cushions through which the springs protruded, a square table, a gas burner and a sink. The stack of newspapers on the table was evidence that the Smiths had remembered the instructions on how to prepare for a home delivery. These were the special hallmark of the Maternity Center. Newsprint is considered to be sterile, something in the ink probably. The doctors were supposed to bake them in the oven until slightly charred, then spread them in the bed under the mother. Some of the papers were to be tightly rolled, and pinned into the bottom sheet at the foot of the bed, as a bar against which the mother could brace her feet. This was the Maternity Center's answer to fancy accommodations.

Separated from the main room by cardboard walls were two small cubicles. In one there was a metal frame bed hidden under a clutter of scattered clothes. A sweater or jacket was occasionally recognizable. This was the communal bedroom for six or more children who slept in a pile sharing warmth and rags. In the other room, a heavy woman, appearing somewhat younger than the man, lay in a sagging bed. She was obviously pregnant. Dozing when the doctors entered, she awakened enough to recognize them, and drifted off again. The husband said this was her sixteenth pregnancy. She had not gone to the Center because she was familiar with the routine. When she felt pains during the night, she knew it was time to call the Center.

Bob began the examination. The blood pressure was 260/120. This was a most unpleasant surprise. In the absence of a prenatal record he could not know if she had been hypertensive, or if this was a recent complication of the pregnancy. He examined her abdomen. The baby was small, but positioned normally. He listened for the fetal heart beat. There was nothing. The baby was dead. Mothers can usually report when they last felt movement, but this woman was confused and not reliable. The findings of elevated blood pressure, dead baby and listless mother strongly suggested toxemia of pregnancy.

The intern confirmed this and agreed that she was not in active labor. The way the rules were written, at this level of care she could not be immediately transferred to a hospital. The intern returned to the Center, leaving Bob to observe the patient.

It was now past noon, and he was hungry. The father directed him to a restaurant a block away. This was a White Tower, a forerunner of McDonalds, taking its name from the tiles which covered it inside and out. Bob had only been in the area a few hours, but the squalor was so oppressive that by contrast this White Tower was the whitest thing he had ever seen. In the same light, the toilet was a marvel of modernism. The food was indifferent, but Bob lingered, reluctant to leave. He returned to the bedside, checked the blood pressure and found no change. He continued through the afternoon. She was not in labor. Children, neighbors and unidentified curious relatives drifted in. Bob was tired. He convinced himself there was no need for a doctor to be there. He asked the father for a phone. It was a block away. Darkness was settling in, changing dreary to menacing. The father led him through an alley, past burned and broken buildings, looking like bombed ruins. The phone had survived, attached to a piece of wall. Bob called the Center praying for someone who could authorize him to leave. A resident was there who had reviewed the intern's report. He supported Bob's conclusion. Bob was to return to the Center and revisit the patient in the morning. He instructed the father to call if anything changed.

During the streetcar ride returning to the Center, Bob dreamed of the luxury of a hot shower, and a quiet bed. Two transfers later he walked into the Center, undressed and fell into bed. Before he was asleep the phone rang. Mrs. Smith-bey had delivered her baby. Bob dressed and rushed out, reversing the streetcar connections he had made an hour earlier. When he arrived at the basement door, he was met not by the father, but confronted by an imposing, middle-aged man, well over six feet, who had a glass in one hand and a bottle of Jim Beam in the other. He poured a drink, gulped it, and with his bottle hand swept back his coat showing a large holstered revolver strapped around his hips. "Ah is Sultan Kulan-bey" he announced. "Ah is heah to protect mah flock."

Bob had no idea what that meant, but he managed to ask, "Protect from what?"

The answer, "From whatever," was not reassuring.

Bob explained that he was the doctor from the Maternity Center, and had been called to see Mrs. Smith-bey.

He was led reluctantly into the bedroom. This was not the same listless scene he had left two hours ago. The mother lay in the sagging bed in a pool of blood that extended from hips to shoulders with a dead baby next to her. She was pale, the unnatural fish gray of black anemia. Sitting in a chair at the foot of the bed was a younger woman who had a definite family resemblance.

Her head was wrapped in a turban fastened by a crescent shaped pin. "Are you a relative?" Bob asked.

"Mah sister," was the sullen answer.

"Let's get this cleaned up. Can you help change the sheets?"

"That is yo doctor's job, not mine."

The lines of responsibility had been clearly defined. There was no time to waste arguing. Bob opened the bag that had been prepared at the Center for normal deliveries, gloves, towels, sutures, simple medications. There was one plasma pack consisting of a bottle of dried plasma and a bottle of saline solution to dissolve it. He connected the two bottles and shook them to mix. He plugged in the tubing and inserted the needle into an arm vein. He was holding the bottle above his head, looking for something to hang it on. He saw a nail in the wall on the opposite side of the room. He asked the Sultan, who was standing in the background, to move the nail closer to the bed. He came in with a large butcher knife and began hammering the nail with the handle. The blade end was slashing near the tubing.

"Don't cut the tube" Bob cautioned.

The Sultan bristled and answered in slurred menacing words, "Ah don't never cut nothin ah don't mean to."

Then he looked down on Bob, barely focusing, and said "Doctor, yo is Jewish."

Realizing that maybe it would be a common bond if they shared discrimination, Bob answered, "Yes," almost eagerly.

The Sultan expanded. "We is brothers. Yo is from the desert of Canaan and ah is from the desert of Moab."

Bob felt very little reassurance.

The supplies in the bag were not adequate for this problem. He needed pitocin to contract the uterus and stop the bleeding. It was nearly midnight. Was there a drug store still open? The father thought there was one about eight blocks away on Division. Bob was not licensed and could not write a prescription, so he would have to go in person and try to convince the pharmacist of the emergency need. He also wanted to call the Center to report, and try to transfer the patient to the County Hospital. The father guided him through the dark ruins. The milky glow from the moth-spattered street lights did little to lessen his fears. Furtive shadows seemed to be everywhere. In this setting Bob would have preferred the hulking Sultan for a guide, but he had sunk into the broken sofa in a drugged sleep. The drug store was open. The pharmacist was unmoved by Bob's appeal, but he was able to call the Center and a resident confirmed the urgency of the need, and gave a prescription by phone. He also agreed to send an ambulance. The father led the return through the same threatening streets, but now the prospect of help made them less ominous.

The mother was now semi-conscious. The room was filled with relatives and neighbors. The women dressed very much alike, loose flowing dresses and turbans, which they considered a proper Muslim uniform for this crisis. They said nothing, but in the silence Bob could feel the threat of what would happen if she died. He injected the pitocin, not knowing if it would really have any effect. Her blood pressure, so high in the afternoon, was not obtainable. The single unit of plasma was finished and disconnected without evidence that it had improved anything. The Sultan rumbled in his stupor. Bob suspected it was beyond alcohol, perhaps syphilitic brain damage. He could be violent if aroused. It was a long hour before the ambulance arrived. A policeman accompanied it as a routine. The attendants loaded the patient and drove away. The scene changed abruptly. After the hours of tension, Bob had been officially relieved of his responsibility. He collected his medical items and repacked the bag. After all the adrenalin, and a gnawing uncertainty that he might not be allowed to leave, he had a sudden weakness, and was eager to get out of the door. Not so. One of the uniformed women appeared with a samovar and made tea. The Sultan sat up and began to clap his hands and shout, rambling in something unintelligible that was supposed to be Arabic. He waved his pistol and carried on in the way he thought a Sultan would. His *ladies* who controlled the streets in the area paid little attention as he continued his fantasy. Smith-bey explained to Bob that this celebration was in his honor because he had saved the life of their beloved sister, so he better look like he was enjoying it.

At the Center the young doctors had been lectured never to eat or drink from any of the dishes. This topped the list of commandments. Bob felt crushed. He was so near to escape and now he was back in the middle of make believe. The ladies passed around the little brass cups that belonged with the samovar. This made everyone feel like a true Arab. Bob asked for a coke, and one was provided. There were little sweet rolls. The ladies sat on the floor in a circle around the Sultan. Bob sat on a milk bottle case. Everyone smiled, and the Sultan closed his eyes and hummed. It was now five o'clock in the morning. Bob was very uncertain how to break away from this ceremony, especially since he was the Honoree, so he simply stood up and walked to the door. No one seemed to notice. One more step and he was out in the awakening sounds of Chicago.

After coffee and a shower he slept until noon. He checked in with the switchboard and began to ready himself for his next turn. He learned that Mrs. Smith-bey had survived. He was thankful, but it was just a thoughtless reflex. There had been so much anxiety and tension that he hadn't really thought of her as a patient, only a problem. As he settled down to wait, the events of the night were already blurred and surreal. Surely it was a dream. He looked through a piece of the Tribune lying there. One small item stood out. During the night a woman had been killed in a lumberyard where he walked. His night indeed had been real.

Chapter 23

Kascht – Remmel

Mr. and Mrs. Norbert Remmel of Hartford, Wisconsin, announce the triumphant impending wedding of their daughter, Miss Mary Ann, to Doctor Robert L. Kascht of Waterloo, Iowa. Doctor Kascht is the son of Mrs. Leo Huntington, prominent matron of Waterloo. She presently is the reigning doyenne of the Elklets in the Waterloo Lodge.

His father, Doctor Lawrence B. Kascht, is gratefully remembered for his enduring dental reconstructions in the towns of Jesup and Brandon, Iowa. His brother, Richard J. Kascht, is currently affiliated with the Rath Meat Packing Company in the capacity of relief salesman, and is now enjoying the ambience of Denver, Colorado. Doctor Kascht was graduated from East Waterloo Iowa High School where he excelled as a cheerleader, class officer, and thespian. He was also active in school publications, the long range planning committee, and was a member of the wrestling team which sent two representatives to the Olympic team of 1940. Following his graduation, he matriculated at the Iowa State Teachers' College, where he achieved on the entrance examination, one of the highest scores in the history of the College. He subsequently served with distinction in the Army Specialized Training Program at Northwestern University Medical School. He interned in Milwaukee, Wisconsin. This was followed by a residency in Internal Medicine at Goldwater Memorial Hospital in New York City. Concurrently he was retained by the Iowa

State Chamber of Commerce to promote the image of the Tall Corn state and impart an appreciation of its culture and sophistication. Following that he returned to Milwaukee, Wisconsin and joined the faculty of Marquette University Medical School, to accept the chair of Anatomy. At present he is also the director of the Department of Pathology at St. Mary's Hospital, Milwaukee. He regularly receives offers from larger institutions, including Sloan-Kettering and the National Cancer Institute, but to date, he has declined because of his dedication to this community. Following his (their) wedding, Doctor Kascht will be at home, and receive guests.

Chapter 24

No Dowry — Not Even a Camel

I married my wife for money. The fact that she was an absolutely gorgeous, black-haired Dresden doll made it easier. Easier, that is, to hide my true motive, because everyone assumed I had just succumbed to obvious physical charm. Not so. I had heard Grandpa Frank repeat it at least a hundred times, "It's just as easy to love a rich one as a poor one," so, subliminally, I was programmed to respond to anyone with money.

I don't know how or why she remained on the open market so long, but she was still available when I finally got around to gambling on a blind date. I knew these were always losers, but what the heck, so I gave it a shot. One of my fellow residents at the hospital was married to a nurse who knew a classmate in nursing school who just happened to be unattached. This is the standard scenario, and it sends up red flags all over the place. The only thing that didn't happen to warn me was the other nurses didn't offer the supportive comment, "The girls all love her." That would have saved me, but no, this guy's wife, true to her role as a young married, had to go through with her unselfish matchmaking to help her friend and me find true happiness.

Accordingly, I was invited to dinner, and discovered I was paired with this lovely little thing who was so artfully designed and equipped to mislead an unwary young man. Doubtless, her mother had urged her directly, and in countless devious ways, ever since puberty, to marry a doctor. She played her role so unobtrusively that

I was not alerted to the danger, and I was passively willing to engage in a temporizing dalliance, as I worked my way along to capturing just the right rich girl.

The dinner went uneventfully, even smoothly. A week or so later I called Mary, that was her name, and arranged a date. She enjoyed the comparative formality of being taken out to dinner. This probably distinguished me from her usual consorts, who risked everything on a hamburger and a movie. After this gambit, things continued along quite peacefully. Mary shared a house with three other girls. This sounded like a very inviting smorgasbord, with the prospect of real home life and home cooking after years of living in hospitals. I discovered almost immediately that the other three were completely taken and beyond my reach, so I concentrated on Mary as my entree to this domestic scene. It was just too good to let it get away. We went out two or three times, and in the course of our small talk I learned that her family owned a nearby small town. This may be a slight exaggeration, it was my own interpretation, but they did own a brewery, a reportedly elegant supper club and a world class ballroom which featured the big bands. This sounded pretty promising. Also, I noticed that Mary wasn't getting any uglier with the passing of time.

About a month after we met something happened. I'm not exactly certain how or what. Anyway, I recall that she prepared Martinis, straight up, for us one evening before we were to go for dinner, but I don't believe we ever ate. About three drinks later I lost clear awareness of what was happening. I know I was standing in the kitchen in the dark and a soft voice was saying sweet things to me.

I took a taxi back to the hospital. The next day I left on a fishing trip. It was a long and hazy ride to the Chippewa Flowage, fortunately with my friend and fellow resident, John Schmitz, doing the driving. After a few days of cold showers, not shaving and smelling like fish, we tired of the wonders of primitive life and returned to civilization.

The very next day Mary called, and questioned where I had been. This should have been a signal, but I didn't read it. Then she came on with something cryptic like, "Mother thinks it's just wonderful."

This had no special meaning to me so I asked, "What does she think is wonderful?"

"About us," she answered.

This was a bit more pointed, but still not clear, so I followed up with, "What about us?"

"You know, about us being engaged."

That did it, that really did it. I yelled something, probably unintelligible, more in pain than a communication.

She went on, "When I told her we were planning an early marriage, she was so excited; the folks want to meet you soon."

The parents weren't all that bad. Mother was an older edition of Mary. She showed us naughty pictures of her flapper days when she was a *Pooh Bah* girl doing the Charleston, and later as a constricted small town socialite living the country club ritual. Norbert was a pleasure. He was an extrovert, gentled by sensitivity and sweet charisma. His smile was an irresistible invitation to join in the fun of living. It exuded from under a nose that was a German version of something between Jimmy Durante and Tony Bennet. Norb booked the big bands, and became buddies with Guy Lombardo, Tommy Dorsey, Kay Kayser and a flock of lesser names. He knew gangster bootleggers, and reportedly made a weekly Chicago run to supply the needs of the monastery at Holy Hill. He played an alto sax and a dirty piano that would have been at home in a New Orleans bawdy house. He was the only son, and inescapably inherited the management of the family enterprises. Unfortunately, his many talents did not include financial smarts, and the empire declined, but through it all, he loved life and had fun.

Mary told me that she was often awakened at two or three in the morning to be shown off when her folks brought home some of the big names for coffee after the dance. She has a sleepy recollection of those names with a few faces attached. On her thirteenth birthday Paul Whiteman presided over her party at the ballroom.

All of this supported my level of aspiration for my future good life. It wasn't Long Island or even Lake Geneva, but it wasn't exactly a pile of chopped chicken livers, either. It was a beginning, and I was reading the **Great Gatsby** for guidance. Grandma Remmel fitted into my picture very nicely. She had a large house filled with oriental rugs and a glut of antiques, silver and glassware that I increasingly coveted, so I worked at impressing her with my knowledge, and appreciation of her good taste. With all this pressure, what could I do? I surrendered.

We were married September 22, 1951, slightly more than four months after we met. My friends were startled and unbelieving because I was known as a deliberate, conservative person who carefully processed every decision. This appeared totally inconsistent, rash and impulsive. Little did they suspect that this was my ultimate calculation. They thought it was just because she was beautiful and congenial. Her folks were faintly concerned with such an impetuous tempo, but she had, after all, captured a doctor who was widely regarded as a very worthwhile person.

The years passed. I became established and increasingly successful. We had four children. We bought a house and a farm, solidified our circle of friends, traveled, educated and launched our children and slipped into stable middle age. All of this time I kept my eyes open, essentially treading water, waiting for an opportunity to improve my lot.

Ostensibly, I supported Mary's development, and encouraged, even trained her, as she began a succession of minor triumphs. She showed considerable competence in response to my efforts, working her way through the chairmanship of the Waukesha Service Club gift shop and Thrift shop. She even came to the point of reliability that I allowed her to balance our checkbook.

The outside world did not realize what a good job I had done. Unfortunately, the Schwartz-Remmel empire had unraveled by the time I came on the scene. Only the shell remained to deceive me. Ironically, the calculation was reversed, I was to be the saviour instead of the beneficiary as I had dreamed. The large breweries were too aggressive and competitive, and there was not yet the sophisticated yuppy market for quality micro-breweries, so the brewery closed. The great war had come, bringing gas rationing, and sobering the national spirit. The draft had siphoned most of the young men. In its wake, recreation patterns changed, new music was born, juke boxes replaced the big bands, the ballroom lost its clientele, and eventually closed. Later in the war, it was used to house German prisoners. Norbert became a car salesman, and Rose traded hauteur for an office desk.

My dreams were shattered, but I have borne this burden of disappointment in silence for forty years, never speaking of it until now. The children are grown, and each is successful in individual ways. The grandchildren are loving, and Mary and I are reasonably happy, using the term broadly, despite my lingering awareness of what might have been.

Our time tape is running on *fast forward*, and one day I may not be talking, or she may not be here listening, so I forgive her for being poor. I would like to tell her, "Thanks a bunch." Maybe it was really true love in disguise.

Chapter 25

The Really Big Computer

Only the very young or the very foolish, think they have planned their lives. This may be a vanity of the proud and successful, but before it is all over, even the mightiest should expect some humbling twists that could not be calculated and controlled. Most of us, at some point in maturing, attribute the course of events, wonderful or malignant, to the alignment of the stars, a mechanistic universe wound like a clock, or the hand of God. Some force beyond ourselves must be given the responsibility, or blame, for what has happened. We need to share this, either in gratitude and wonder, or in anger and resentment.

With this orientation, I accept that I had very little to do with the happenings that comprised my life. I was the one who made the trip, and I often thought I had a hand on the tiller, but at the most, I was only trying to adjust to the crossing winds that tossed and buffeted me. I contributed only small details and a little flavoring. I did not plan to be a physician. I gave lip service to my mother's frequently expressed expectation, and enrolled in college as a pre-med. This was really to avoid selecting a major so I could explore more widely, and escape a tunnel vision of the world. The underlying impulse, always near the level of consciousness, was to get somewhere beyond the grayness of poverty, sickness and the meat packing plant. I entered the army, was sent to medical school and followed on that course. I made some compass readings, and veered occasionally, but the big events just happened in an unreasoned way. It has always been jarring to look back and appreciate the orderly sequencing, and the apparently causal relationship, of having been at a specific point at just the right time so the next destined thing could happen.

I got as far as medical school with the helpful pressure of the army. It was expected to be a long war and doctors would be needed. I actually have the illusion it was my own merit that enabled me to get into Northwestern University. So much for that. Whatever. When the war ended, I was discharged from the army. I was in my senior year, and applying for an internship. As a new civilian, I chose to relax after three years of continuous school, and get a job for a few months. I went to Spokane and worked in a sawmill. One day I received a telegram from the assistant dean informing me that I had not been accepted for the internship I had expected. This was more than just a speed bump; it was disruptive.

I rushed back to Chicago to make alternative arrangements. To clarify what had happened, the dean guardedly hinted that at the next interview I would do well to work in subtly the fact that I was German and Catholic. Reportedly, I had been rejected because it was assumed I was Jewish. One of my classmates said his father was the chief of staff at a hospital in Milwaukee, and he could arrange an interview for me. At this late stage I had very little choice. I had never been to Milwaukee, but I applied by phone and went for an interview. I was accepted. Everything in my life was obviously contingent on this almost trivial event. If I been tall and blond, with a simple name like Smith, none of it would have happened, and I would never have met my Wisconsin-born wife. For better or worse, the scenario would have played with a different cast and setting.

Later in my internship, I began planning for a residency. I didn't have a well-defined preference, but Internal Medicine seemed to be broad and unconfining, so I decided to try that. One of my classmates was interning in New York. He wrote that there was a residency available in Physical Medicine at his hospital, and this would be a way of getting started. This seemed somewhat tangential, but plausible, so I called, and was invited to come for an interview. I rode the Pacemaker overnight and was welcomed graciously. After the interview, I went to meet the head of the Physical Medicine department at his office in the McGraw Hill building. This was big time to a farm boy, just recently graduated from school. Then the details began to emerge. I was to be the live-in personal resident for this doctor's practice, which consisted predominantly of society alcoholics. My duties would be to supervise the administration of IV fluids, vitamins and sedatives for this select clientele, and be discreet and supportive. The educational benefits of this arrangement were minimal. However, he hinted that if it worked out well, I might eventually join his group. The war had given a great boost to the specialty of Physical Medicine, and I thought I might really develop an interest in it. I would receive residency credit and a modest salary, and I would have the opportunity to become acquainted with the important names in New York medical circles. It was appealing for these reasons, but the sense of being exploited outweighed them. To his surprise I refused. I believe he thought I was ungrateful.

I returned to the hospital, and told the director of graduate training I thought it was disgraceful for the hospital to waste an approved residency in such a questionable collusion. I also said things about the hospital educational system prostituting itself for obvious financial gain. I vigorously expressed my indignation at the whole scheme, and the waste of my time and money. When I returned to Milwaukee, a telegram was waiting for me, asking that I contact the education director of the hospital. I called and was greeted with surprising warmth, and offered a residency in Medicine at one of the city hospitals. The director told me that the committee had been so impressed with my integrity, that they would have liked to give me a residency, but there were none available, so they arranged for the one that was offered to me. I accepted with gratitude. I went to the big city, remained essentially a small town boy, and did well. It is a privilege to be a physician, and I have had many rewarding experiences. They go with the job, and no physician should feel important, just favored. I make an exception of this episode in my early years, and feel quietly proud.

Chapter 26

The Year I Missed Christmas

I have been writing and rewriting this in my mind for almost fifty years. Ever since it happened in 1953, I have wanted to tell someone, to talk about it. I just wanted to know if it was real. Through all that time I drifted in and out, did it actually happen like I remember? It would have been therapeutic to hear myself talk, but I couldn't do it. I was frightened. At first I was afraid I would get a bad conduct discharge. That would have ruined my life. Then I thought, even worse, the Air Force might not discharge me, but keep me in and under control. If I said the wrong things, they could retaliate and blame me for what had happened. I imagined I could be locked up, or hidden away. Then as time passed, and I was living an ordinary life, I began to worry that someone might find out. I was ashamed. At times I panicked. Once I was lecturing, very coherently I thought, really on a roll. As I glanced around the class in the amphitheater, I noticed a young man who wasn't paying attention. He was reading something. Was he aware that I wasn't qualified to give this lecture? What would he do? I went on automatic pilot, turned off the lights and began to project slides and ask questions. I got by that time, but I was spooky ever after, waiting for something to go wrong, for someone to sense I wasn't really under control. For the rest of these fifty years, I have leaked by, without anyone seeing through my veneer. I was quite competent and effective, but I sweated inside. I have accepted my limitations. I have been very disciplined and deliberate.

I developed little artifices and tricks. I rehearsed everything I did, every lecture, every trip, even social activities. I always arrived early so I could familiarize myself with the setting. I was never spontaneous. I couldn't risk making a mistake with everyone watching. I learned to live with a flawed self-image, but I have disappointed myself. I know I settled for less than I might have been.

Last week my wristwatch slowed down, losing five minutes a day. I took it in for cleaning, and I recalled I had bought it at the PX in the days when all of this started. It really seems a short time ago, but the watch forcefully reminded me it was fifty years, and if I want my family to know about this, I better get to writing. I don't know why that is so important. I suppose I want to justify myself, and perhaps create a softer image for them. The impact of this episode in shaping and distorting my life was second only to the long illness and death of my father during the early days. It has been an unwanted phantom, a nagging whisper, eroding my self-esteem and gnawing at every achievement. This has been the determining force through most of my adult life.

Anyway, I am now committed to sharing this. The problem is where to start, and as usual, the words of Alice come to mind: "Begin at the beginning."

ଽଚ୪

From early childhood until I was married, I never felt much affection. Despite all the effort my mother put into making a sense of family for us, it was just survival. We laughed some, and we had fun times, but it was only temporary. My father had TB and we knew he was dying. It just took a long time, but we had to go on day after day pretending it wasn't so. Anything we did wasn't for real. It would come to an end when he died. Inevitably time passed and we grew older. We worked and went to school, and came home, and made meals, and shined our shoes, and went to church, and cleaned house and did laundry, and made a few friends. None of that meant much, because we knew, bone deep, that it wouldn't last. Eventually it happened, he died, but even when it was over, it really wasn't over. Things hadn't changed much. We still did the same things, and carried along the same feelings. We didn't know how to be any different. In a way we were free now, but we had the same outlook, nothing very good was going to happen, and anyway it wouldn't last. On the outside we looked like ordinary people, poor, clean, hardworking, honest, a real-life Horatio Alger poster family. On the inside we were struggling not to be dreary. Mother was heroic. She had kept his dishes separate, boiled them in Lysol water, and did his laundry separately for almost seven years. My brother and I were not allowed to enter his room in all that time. It was a triumph of careful hygiene. We did not become ill. After his death, mother worked in a lady's dress shop, was a jewelry clerk in a department store, drove around in our old Essex, trying to collect overdue accounts for a pharmacist, and she even sold homemade furniture polish, walking from door to door. Finally, she bluffed her way into becoming a self-annointed dental assistant. She did this for years. None of us ever gave much thought to all of this, and she didn't dramatize the situation. I don't think she had any broad perspective or self-awareness that could reassure her for how much she did. She was so habituated through the years of gray routine that she had no vision of a better way. Life just ground on. Eventually circumstances improved and she married again.

I was fifteen. In my memories, it seems that she didn't really know what I was all about. She encouraged my unrealistic hope of going to college. Somehow she came to the conclusion that Bob was going to be a *Doctor.* She said it in a reverential tone. From that first realization, she supported and urged, with a closed mind. As she said about many of her opinions, "It's a known fact," and in her mind it became so. It was the period in my life for change, for germination, and I went along an undramatic course that provided an escape. I graduated from high school, attended college and worked second shift in a meat packing plant, enlisted in the army after Pearl Harbor and finally, fulfilling mother's forecast, the army sent me to medical school. This was followed by a residency in Internal Medicine in New York, graduate school at Marquette, Pathology residency at St. Mary's, and marriage.

The second fifteen years of my life were as simple and linear, as deterministic, as the first half had been. At one time when I still thought I was destined to be a literature professor, I read Joyce's *"Portrait of an Artist as a Young Man."* I picked up the phrase: "Arbeit und rhythmus," and for years I thought this exactly expressed the unplanned happenings of my life, putting one foot ahead of the other, until I was wherever I was. After I married, I realized I was in a stable state. Surprisingly, I was actually happy, and I had a reasonable expectation of a good tomorrow. That was fleeting, and true to past experiences, things changed, of course for the worse. It was during the Korean War, and the armed forces were short of doctors. The solution was easy, a selective draft of physicians, especially those who had been educated at government expense. Everyone who was in this vulnerable category protested that it was like any other assignment. One went where he was sent, for the greater needs of the service. This logic and eloquence was lost in the bureaucratic mill. I was ordered to apply for a commission or be drafted, so I did.

I became a captain, and traveled to Gunter Air Force base in Montgomery where I magically became both an officer and a gentleman. This was a modern Tower of Babel. Physicians from all parts of the country were there. In their varied accents, and with their distinctive mannerisms, they resented being impressed into service, shanghaied, conscripted and discriminated against. They protested loudly and at length. Many of them knew a congressman who was working on their case, and they expected to be returned to their normal lives and careers by the next mail. They were indignant, furious, violated and outraged by this breach of their constitutional guarantees. I, without such privileged connections, was quietly lost. I was back fifteen years when things happened without reason, and I was tossed without my consent and to no purpose. I had no control. This was a six week program. Most of the others settled in. They did normal things, drinking, partying and getting acquainted with the nurses, who, for whatever reasons, had also joined the Air Force. I often recall this enclave of disparate mavericks when I watch the reruns of *M*A*S*H*. Then one day we received our assignments. This union of outraged misfits was fragmented, divided into those who had it good and those who were going to purgatory. All former alliances and strategies were deleted. Those assigned to Saudi Arabia threatened to convert to Judaism so they could claim religious exemption. The *Chosen Ones*, destined for Germany, were elated, but most found it prudent not to flaunt their good fortune. A few weeks earlier all energies were focused on getting out of the service; now it was more immediate and pragmatic to try to get reassigned. Without recourse, I was assigned to Chateauroux, France.

My initial reaction was quite peaceful. I had my high school French to show off, and I had read French in graduate school. I was ready for culture to happen to me, haut cuisine and vintage wine. In the following days the rumor mill ground at full speed. The men assigned to bases in the states were annoyed and grumbled about the interruption of their personal plans just to go and treat dependents who should be seen by the local doctors in their area. Anyone going to Saudi or Tripoli was too depressed to share in the chatter. The Germany contingent tried to look sympathetic for the less fortunate, but it was annoying and patronizing. I was in the uncertain group, what did we know about Chateauroux? I felt comfortable with my simple image of France from travelogues and movies, and my mock Charles Boyer accent. Of course this didn't hold up against the flow of real world reports. They weren't grim like the news from North Africa, but negative, glum and certainly not appealing. It was well established that the French didn't like Americans. I assumed this was like most generalizations, but I found it was essentially true. There was a national neurosis of subconscious resentment against the men who twice had rescued them from the Germans. Much more disturbing to me was the problem with housing. There were no government quarters. One had to rent from the locals and live off the base. This was a time of considerable French communist activity, and I feared it would be difficult for Mary.

The six weeks finally ended. We had learned how to wear the uniform, and the organization and mission of the Air Force was explained to us. Presumably we were prepared to go forth and do our duty. Unfortunately, we had no esprit de corps. We did not develop a cohesive sense of pride. It was just drudging servitude. I don't remember a single doctor from that experience. My most vivid recall is of the major, reportedly a green beret, who stomped into the classroom and passed around a tin of *peanuts*. We were free to eat them during his lecture. After we had done so, he told us that this was a class in jungle survival and those were fried grubworms. What a stupid memory to represent this period of my life. There wasn't any warm and meaningful final ceremony. This wasn't a graduation, it was a diaspora. We just went on our separate ways. I drove to Wisconsin. Mary and little Larry were staying with her folks. We did a lot of hugging, I said goodbye, and took the train to the embarkation port. I endured intimate sharing with eight other officers in a crowded unventilated cabin for the next fourteen days, but I couldn't complain, because it was so much better than the accommodations of the two thousand enlisted men in the lower decks. I didn't get seasick. I just had a continuing headache, and a gnawing sense of greater distance and separation with every passing day. Mostly I sat on deck and looked at the water. I became increasingly anxious about what was coming, and dreaded the end of the voyage. We landed in Bremerhaven, the port from which my German ancestors had sailed in the 1850's. I boarded a train to France. It was an unusual type of sleeping car, an alternate head to foot arrangement of casket-like compartments. I slept very poorly. I was wakened at 2A.M. by loud laughter and talking at a small station where we stopped. I knew from my stereotype that we were in France. "It was a known fact," that they were loud. This was the welcome to my new home.

⁊

The base was a twenty minute jeep ride from the station. The young airman who came for me gave a rambling commentary, like a trainee for a Grayline tour. It was very informative, but it wouldn't have been endorsed by either the local Chamber of Commerce or the Air Force. He was very chatty, enjoying the private one-on-one talk with an officer. I also sensed that he was giving me a bit of shock therapy.

He ventured to inquire, "How come you got to a place like this?" I interpreted this as meaning, *"What did you do to get shipped here?"*

My official orientation packet described it as the second largest supply base in the free world, after Wright- Patterson. It was officially designated as Chateauroux Air Depot, familiarly known as CHAD. My guide volunteered his opinion that the stupid place would never be completed because the U.S. government had an agreement with the French to use only hand labor. He identified it as *manoover* which apparently was the GI version of *main oeuvre.* Anyway it was pronounced, it meant that a battalion of Army engineers, with earth moving equipment, was sitting by watching while the Frenchmen and Arabs dug with shovels. As I observed this in practice during the following months, it seemed to be a clever way of solving the local unemployment problem, worthy of a French diplomat. The travelogue focused on a cluster of crumbling buildings that looked like a school or barracks, about midway between town and the base, where the local cell of communists gathered. I was told of their annoying practice of shutting off the electric power to the base, just to prove they could do it. The roadside was cluttered with small auto vans, where the business girls lived. The airman asked if I wanted to stop and be introduced. As we neared the main gate he told me that the base was so big that much of the stuff stored there was already lost, without inventory records. He dropped me off at the front door of the hospital where I was to report.

A bored airman ushered me into the office of Lt. Colonel Paul Davis M.D., commanding officer of the 73rdUSAF hospital. He was hunched over his desk, arms spread, looking as if he had been caught napping. He was in the early fifties, appropriately streaked with gray. He slightly resembled Walter Pidgeon. At one time he might have been handsome, but *puffy* and *florid* had replaced that, and tarnished his appeal. His macho was overripe and gone to seed. It was evident he had pursued promotions more vigorously at Happy Hour than at the hospital. I gave my best fresh-out-indoctrination salute and handed over my envelope of orders. He responded with his listless version, and waived me to a chair. He glanced at them, and then tried a welcoming speech. "We have been expecting you. Pathologists aren't very common. We are planning great things here. This hospital will be the largest in the European command, of course after the headquarters at Wiesbaden. We will process all the referrals from the North African bases." He sounded like he had been programmed and repeated this a dozen times a day. I couldn't sense if he believed it. As he spoke he gently stroked his little mustache, hoping to be debonair, but it didn't work. He just looked used and beefy. "When you leave tell the airman out there to get the lab sergeant to show you around. Don't forget, sick call starts at O-eight-hundred hours." I got up, saluted, did an about face and left. I was dismayed that the Pathologist, the crowning dollop on this man's dream cake, would be expected to do sick call.

The clerk called the lab and in a few minutes I met the man who would be my closest associate, Staff Sergeant Shafford Archer. We measured each other for a long minute. Archer knew the system had decreed that I was in charge. I had seen enough Sgt. Bilko skits to realize that this was nonsense. We saluted, at the same time. I would have preferred a handshake. He said, "Sir, I am here to help you." It was either a genuine, gracious offer, or it was a proper military gesture that hid a load of disdain. I very much preferred to have a friend. Archer was a Southerner. This was of no significance, just a fact. He was slightly younger than I, and had been in the Air Force six years. Very likely, this would be a career for him. He was pleasant looking and unremarkable, but he gave the impression of being a bit devilish, possibly because he was Irish. Under his guidance I began my second travelogue of the day. First we went to the barracks. The room I was assigned would have fitted in an average Y in the States. It was drab and without amenities. I couldn't think of enjoying living there. I left my hand luggage, and we moved on to the lab. It was two rooms and three airmen. One room had sitdown desks, presumably for doing blood counts. The other had standup cabinets suitable for chemistry and bacteriology. There was a sparse mixture of glassware that must have been adequate for the work volume. In one corner was a desk with a microscope. Obviously, this was for me. It was a disheartening introduction to the reality of Chateauroux. Most of the doctor's offices at home were better equipped. I felt like an engineer who had just been given a toy erector set. There was one startling item, completely out of place. On a separate table was an Autotechnicon. This is a marvel of automation, consisting of a timing mechanism that advances samples of tissue through a sequence of solutions, preparing them to be examined microscopically. It is the most distinctive icon of the Pathology laboratory. This instrument and I were equal partners in a charade; we were supposed to add credibility to the pretense that this hospital would someday be a medical center. I asked Archer about it. He said it had arrived six months ago, but no one had touched it since it was unpacked. We walked through the other buildings. Probably forty beds were ready and operational, but there were few patients. This was a healthy subset of the population, and except for trauma and hernias, there wasn't much to do. I quickly calculated how many books I would have time to read in the next twenty months. I could be very learned, but I didn't see that many books. There were six or eight buildings. We walked through each of them. They were unfinished, and smelled like paint and plaster. The windows were smeared with putty, and still had stickers on them. The buildings were cement block, covered with stucco and painted glaring white. Between the buildings the soil was deeply gouged. No attempt had been made to soothe the ravages of construction. This was the clay that had been churned for two millennia by marching feet, from the days of the Roman legions to the American infantry. It was impervious and retained permanent pools of water. Any thought of grading or planting would be negotiated in the distant future, doubtless by another session of Congress.

Next, Archer drove around the base, and through the depot storage areas. This was the fun part of the trip. He had an MG two seater. It was his passion. He certainly knew more about cars than he did about medical lab work. He tuned and tinkered in most of his free time. As we drove, Archer gave me a measured discussion of the base. He was less gossipy than the airman who brought me from the train. A sergeant was expected to have a more reserved manner, and he was cagey enough at this stage of our relationship not to gamble with my confidences, but I got much the same message from the airman and the sergeant: the place was a disaster, and what was I doing here? He dropped me at the building that housed the so-called officer's club and dining room. I met a few people, but I was too tired and scrambled to remember much, and I went to bed. I had survived day one, only about seven hundred to go.

The night ended, and I got up. I had swirled in and out of half-sleep and delirium, with the colonel's words chasing me, like a repeating echo, "Don't forget sick call." The last weeks were blurred; I was in a trance, dragged and tossed five thousand miles from home, then dumped into a muddle of strangers. Breakfast was in the all purpose officer's club. I forced myself to go. In the morning it was heavy with smells of left over drinks and sour metallic cigar smoke. It lacked the chatter and jukebox that made it almost tolerable at night. Breakfast was a fixed menu, *oeufs avec jambon*. This was served on aluminum pie tins. The eggs were fried and had been waiting for me until the tops dried. The toast was charred and cold. It wasn't the *petit déjeuner* shown in travel folders. Everyone was rushing to get to sick call. An officer next to me identified the Catholic chaplain who had just entered, bleary, tousled and unshaved. For my orientation he commented that he must have had a bad time with his girl last night. When I asked what he meant, he told me that the priest lived with a woman in town. That jolted me. Deep in my jangled mind I had a faint idea that if things really got too much for me, I could always go see the chaplain. This was the common wisdom, but it didn't survive the reality of this setting. My champion and counselor was gone. I followed along to sick call. My experience as a medical resident had put me in the New York city welfare clinics where people were really sick. They ranged from ordinary heart failure to leprosy. Nothing had prepared me for this. It was like running the gauntlet. The doctors had to survive getting past the patients. Airmen slouched against the walls or sprawled on the floor with legs sticking out at all angles to be stumbled over. They pushed and punched each other. They mumbled and grumbled. No one was in a hurry. This was time off. Occasionally a sergeant yelled, "At Ease," and it had a brief effect. I made it through as part of the team on offense, and was shown to a curtained cubicle. My one interesting patient had venereal warts. I had never seen this. It wasn't part of my world, but it became routine here. I asked the neurologist next to me what to do. He said, "That brown bottle on your table is podophyllin. Swab some on the warts". I did. Unfortunately, he hadn't cautioned me to use it sparingly. The next morning a very agitated airman was looking for me, and exhibited a painful, swollen member of his anatomy. Other than this, there was nothing I saw or did that wouldn't have been within the capability of an Eagle Scout. After all the malingerers were cleared out and forced back to duty, at about 10:30, I went to the lab, my home base. It was quiet. No one was calling for a report. No one complained that something hadn't been collected or done. There were no frozen sections scheduled for surgery. The two lab techs didn't have a problem, no unidentified blood cells or a test that didn't go right. That was simply because there wasn't much of anything being done. There wasn't a doctor waiting in my so-called office to review an algorithm on the workup for porphyria, or a discussion of the bone marrow findings in a case of acute leukemia I had just diagnosed. No, there was none of that. The airmen were content with their routine and I knew enough not to jiggle it. I read a while, walked around and tried to find something to do. I reminded myself every so often that this was the first day of the rest of my life. That was the goody-goody axiom to inspire a full appreciation of each moment, and not to waste a precious one. It fell flat. I soon discovered that this random day was a perfect sample to represent all the other days. I couldn't conceive of seven hundred more of the same. Inevitably days and weeks passed. I became acquainted with my fellow physicians. They were an ordinary mix. Most of them were specialty board eligible. Those who were certified, were in Wiesbaden. Being second level, we had this common bond for our paranoia and resentment. There were fourteen men who represented most of the specialties. Everyone shared sick call, and tried to collect an occasional specialty referral. Certainly, the busiest were the urologist and the psychiatrist. Understandably, the circumstances provided them abundant patients. The surgeons also had a steady supply from accidents and fights. Otherwise it was basically a healthy group with very little disease variety. I had expected exotic things, maybe an occasional African parasite, a schistosome or some malaria. I never saw either. The urologist was bored with the excess of VD. It was undramatic and monotonous, and he just gave shots. The psychiatrist was a very peaceful guy. In later years I compared him to Sidney Friedman in the *M*A*S*H* series. He was a loose, slack and relaxed Scotsman, named Dave McDonald. Before I met him, I assumed the word *dour* was invented for the Scots, but he was the very opposite. At first, I had some uncertainty being with him. I knew I looked and acted unhappy. I thought this was justified, and I didn't make any pretense of hiding it, but I did wonder occasionally if this qualified as depression. I didn't know what this meant, but it sounded ominous, and maybe something that would arouse a more professional interest. I talked with him a few times about it, but he wasn't excited, and seemed to dismiss it as a reasonable reaction to my status as overqualified and underutilized.

I believe Colonel Davis tried to ignore me because of a faint awareness of the ridiculous situation. He was officious and rough with most of the officers, criticizing and nagging in an unpredictable and petty way. He made an inspection of the hospital once a week, usually on Friday, although this might change just to add a bit more annoyance. It was his conception of the way things were done in the military, but it was a caricature. He grumbled and barked. Everyone went through the proper motions of responding and answering with a "Sir," then the inspection team moved on. In the laboratory there was very little to check. He wasn't qualified to deal with quality control, or a standard deviation, or the technical procedures, and mostly there wasn't anything to see except the glassware. He regularly stopped at the Autotechnicon and said, "Doctor, we have to get this going soon." I could feel him give it a mental pat. He was satisfied with this proof that we were going to do great things. One day he said, "I think you better go TDY to Wiesbaden and see if you can figure out some way for us to start doing our own surgical pathology here." I didn't have any idea what that meant. All the directives I knew about said that surgical specimens would be sent to the headquarters hospital for examination and diagnosis, and that is exactly what we did. What kind of wild errand would I be on trying to reverse that? I had orders in two days and flew to Wiesbaden. I met my counterpart at the hospital. This was the position I would have liked. The pathologist wasn't interested in my problems. He had no idea how we could share the work, and he definitely didn't want competition. After two days of the good life, German food and beer, and the heady sight of a busy laboratory where there was a semblance of medical science, I was on my way back to nowhere. I realized I was a captive in the table of organization. I told the colonel there was only one solution, transfer me, either to Wiesbaden or to England, where there were some quality facilities. He was very much agitated. I had injected a hard note of reality that threatened his dream world.

After this brief skirmish, trying to make an end run, I realized I was in my permanent assignment. I began making gross descriptions of the surgical specimens. It was unofficial, redundant and possibly contrary to some sacred regulation, but it gave me a sense of satisfaction. My *diagnoses* on these simple specimens were usually as accurate as the official ones that came two weeks later. I questioned the married men about housing arrangements. I learned there was a complex of old buildings in which some Americans lived. It had a quaint name, Chateauneuf. There is a well known wine by that name, but I think it was somewhere else. These buildings dated from the time of WWI. It was possible to buy an apartment unit for $1200. That was a considerable sum. I didn't have that much, but Mary's folks could get it if necessary. This certainly wasn't an ideal solution. The housing was twenty miles from the base, and I didn't have a car. In final resignation, I bought a unit, and started the application for Mary to join me.

I tried to adjust and fit into the group. I went to town occasionally, either on the bus or with one of the men who had a car. One evening some of them asked me to go along for dinner. I didn't have much feeling for most of them, but I needed contact and some activity, so I went. I don't remember the meal, but afterwards, the urologist, who was at the top of my non-favorites list, suggested that they go to a bar with a brothel. I panicked. I had no way to get back to the base. I didn't even know where I was in the town. I ran off down the street, looking for a taxi. I didn't find one. I probably was shouting. There were no street lights. I saw a light. It was a bar, and a jeep driven by MP'S had just arrived to stop a fight. I begged for a ride. It wasn't allowed, but they must have recognized my condition, and since they were taking a drunken airman back to the base, they agreed to let me ride along. I didn't recover completely from that, and rarely went to town unless I was certain of a return ride. This episode increased my separation from the others, and made me feel even more alone.

I didn't write much to Mary. It was extremely painful to get into a reverie, focused on her, talking as though we were together, almost to reach out to touch her, and then realize where we were. It was simpler just to let her fade and rest on another plane. More than that, I didn't want to leak any of the flavor of Chateauroux through my letters. I did send an exciting account of my Wiesbaden visit. She could hear the Oompah Bands in it. It is a truth I have confirmed many times throughout my life: when you most need to do something, it is the most difficult. This is even true for praying. Apart from the personal inadequacies, and the sensitivity I brought to the situation, CHAD was a drab place. It was not a recruiting showpiece. The mission wasn't the *sky blue yonder*. It was supply, and the men stationed there had the self-image of factory workers. This even came off on the medical personnel. I more or less settled in, like a tire adjusting to running on a wheel out of line. The days passed, and at times I would count, only six hundred more to go. There was a bravado slogan: *I can do that standing on my head.*

I performed two autopsies, which in the colonel's mind, probably justified my assignment. The first was a pilot who had ejected from his failing plane and fell to the earth without his parachute opening. It had been determined that he had not jettisoned the seat, which in those days wasn't automatic; it required the pilot to do it after he was out of the plane. With seat still attached, the chute couldn't open properly, and seat and pilot tumbled down in a tangle. I found that he had only one coronary artery. The stress testing available at that time had not detected it. I postulated this had decreased his cardiac reserve. He blacked out and was unable to clear the seat. I was an instant, but momentary, success for this concise analysis that relieved the Air Force of its problem. Certainly, that was why I was there.

The second was less dramatic, but more interesting from the medical view. A mechanic died, without obvious cause. He had been an annoyance, continually on sick call, complaining of headaches. This was especially confusing because he repeatedly explained that the only relief he could obtain was to lie under the plane engine and reach up to work on some part. It was a small step for his superiors, and even the casual medical comment, to connect the complaint and the cure to his need for a security blanket. The psychiatrist was not an official consultant to this conclusion. My examination of his brain revealed a colloid cyst of the third ventricle. It was pedunculated, and could move and block the flow of fluid. I suggested that when he lay on his back with neck arched, the tumor repositioned and the fluid pressure was relieved. I thought this logic was as brilliant as the first one, but it didn't generate much official recognition.

My final success was extremely difficult for me. An Air Force plane had crashed in Paris, and I, the official pathologist for France, was ordered to perform the autopsy examinations on the flight crew. I was flown to Paris by a very nervous pilot who knew of the purpose for my special flight. He commented a number of times, that if the word got out what I was doing, they would have a *walking air force.* I was to work at the American Hospital. The six bodies were there in the morgue. It was reported to me that the plane had just flown from the States and was circling over Paris taking pictures. This plane was a C-119, the one known for its twin tails. Presumably, the side cargo door had been opened for a better view. It somehow became detached, blew off and damaged the tail assembly. The plane spiraled down out of control, crashed and burned. The examination was a ghoulish experience. I have no idea what meaningful information it provided, but it was another of the service duties dictated by regulations. The men were standing, knees bent, as if they were braced for a shock. The uniforms were completely burned. The skin was charred and burned. Most of the muscles were exposed, and very much resembled the plates in an Anatomy Atlas, with the muscle groups clearly defined. The tissues were almost impossible to cut. I didn't know what to do. I believe I stayed six days. I examined one body a day, trying to do the routine, but it was futile. I retreated to my hotel room at night, almost hiding, and wrote the reports. I had no curiosity to see Paris. The one pleasant memory, I saw General Gunther, the Supreme Commander of all forces in Europe, in the lobby. I thought of rushing to him and asking for reassignment.

I flew back to Chateauroux, in more of a haze than before. I heard no comments about my special duty assignment. The reports probably went into a permanent file, gathered dust, and the government paid death benefits. I continued my non-essential routine. One duty was added. The colonel became concerned about the cleanliness of an ice cream vendor who drove his little truck to the main gate of the hospital compound and sold cones. We must determine if this was a possible source of food poisoning. I was ordered to sample and culture this, and report to the colonel. My logic was that he was French, so the product very likely wasn't pristine, and what difference did it make. The GI's ate the same stuff all over town and we hadn't had a diarrhea epidemic, so instead of swabs and culture plates and maybe triggering an international incident, I simply bought a cone, ate it and if things went uneventfully, I sent the report to the colonel, "No problems with the ice cream." It was gratifying. I was back in grade school, sticking out my tongue. Eventually he lost interest. This episode resembled the strawberries problem in the recently published book, **The Caine Mutiny.**

One carefree memory remains as a souvenir. I went to Paris

with two congenial outcasts. I hoped it would replace my first image and memories. For a weekend I was buddies with the veterinarian, the official custodian of foods and sanitation, and the Protestant chaplain. We *did* the Louvre, and all the tourist places, and we ate eggs scrambled with brains and buerre noire for breakfast, and we visited Notre Dame for mass, but we couldn't see the altar because all the devout were standing around reading the news or a racing form. We climbed on the parapets and took pictures of each other among the gargoyles. Most distressing, I discovered that the *ladies* roaming the Champs Elysees, tugged at the chaplain more energetically than they did me. I suspect a chaplain was a greater trophy than a mere doctor would have been, but it might have been because he was a very striking looking man. We thought we were the most rollicking trio to threaten Paris since Dumas introduced the original musketeers. This ended and we returned to our real world. Mary was scheduled to come, but it would be in the new year. I still had to buy a car. My life seemed to be in a steady state, however that might be defined. I have no idea that I was different in any way from what I was a month or two earlier.

℠)Й℟

Two days before Christmas, December 23rd, the colonel called me into his office, and in a husky, nervous voice said, "Come with me." He walked across the hall into a vacant storage room. An airman was there, and an MP came in after I did.

"Take off your clothes."

"What? What kind of nonsense is that?" I was too surprised to be frightened.

He spoke louder, "If you don't do it, I'll have the airman undress you."

I began to yell, "What's wrong, what did I do?" I began to take off my uniform, there seemed to be no alternative. It was so unreal, I just went with the order. I was standing in my shorts.

He said, "Stick your arms straight out in front of you".

Again I just did it because I didn't know what else to do. Instantly the airman stepped in front of me, slipped a straight jacket over my arms, and in one motion crossed them over my chest. The MP pulled the sleeves around to the back and buckled them.

The colonel said, "That's good, now lie down on the stretcher." I couldn't, but by now I was so agitated and disoriented I didn't know what I was doing. The MP picked me up and laid me on the stretcher and strapped me on. I was crying, but I tried to make sense.

"Colonel, what's this all about?"

He bent over, face close to mine, and said, "Doctor, you are sick. I am transferring you to the Psych ward at Wiesbaden. You will get good care."

I asked, "Did Dr. McDonald say that? Why doesn't he tell me that? Couldn't he help me?"

"Our psychiatrist is gone for the holidays, but one of our internists signed your papers. You were reported to be discussing suicide, and we can't be too careful."

I yelled a denial, but he just bent over again, and with sly satisfaction, he said, "I'm no psychiatrist, but I can tell you, your reaction to all this is abnormal. You have shallow affect. Don't you think a normal guy would have been fighting and swearing?"

I remember wondering how he had come up with a term like that. It was beyond his usual insight. It sounded like something he read in a manual. I did argue, and asked him what he would have thought if I had been violent. Suppose I was raving and screaming. That certainly would have confirmed his conclusion, but this was no time for logic. He was pleased with himself. This had gone so smoothly. I was given a sedative, but my adrenaline was more than a match for that, and I stayed awake and troubled throughout the trip. I was carried to an ambulance and driven across the base to the flight line. The airman rode with me. One plane, an old reliable C-47 was sitting there warming up. The stretcher and I were carried on and fastened down. The pilot finished his cigarette, and got in the cockpit, grumbling that this wasn't in his Christmas plans. At Wiesbaden the process was reversed. I was placed in an ambulance, and with more drama, driven to the 7100 USAF Hospital. We drove as if it were an emergency, with the *klaxon* on full volume. European emergency vehicles didn't have sirens like those in the States. This was different. It was an intermittent, harsh sound, something like barking, very insistent. It demanded attention, and was especially jarring, listening from the inside, knowing I was the center of all the commotion. I was unloaded at the hospital and taken to Ward 6B.

I was unstrapped, lifted from the stretcher and the jacket removed. A locked room was enough security to protect the interests of the Air Force. I had never thought what it would be like to be imprisoned. I felt a surge of panic, something like claustrophobia, I imagine. I could have pounded on the door and screamed, but I didn't. I thought of the colonel's observation, that I had shallow affect, and I wondered if I really should be wild. The psychiatrist was gone for the holidays. It seemed odd to me, and very inconvenient, that my only hope for a reprieve depended on a Jew who was celebrating Christmas. He would be gone for four days. During that time I was kept in the *Secure Ward*, as it was properly called. I didn't have shoelaces. I didn't shave although a nurse did shave me once. I ate off pie tins with a plastic spoon. I pretended to listen to a well-intentioned group singing carols, to provide a sense of the spirit of Christmas. I very much wanted to do the *normal* thing, whatever that was. I observed that most of the others in the ward didn't seem crazy, whatever I might have expected. It concerned me, that maybe I wasn't any different from them. I went to CRAFT twice a day. This was the ultimate therapy, to reconnect me with some interest. I chose to work with leather. I was given a rectangle of thick cow's hide. I soaked it overnight. Then I punched holes around the margins so I could lace it together. I was given a punch that had a variety of rosette heads, so I could hammer and imprint the wet leather. It came out quite well, looking somewhat floral. It dried, and I finished it with a dark decorative plastic lace. Polishing used up hours. This wallet is in the back of a dresser drawer. No one has seen it. I would have thrown it away, but it has acquired a perverse value, confirming that I really did have this experience.

The second day after Christmas Dr. Harold Davidson returned. He worked his way through the stack of admissions, and eventually came to me. He stormed into the ward, introduced himself, asked what kind of idiocy this was, and released me from the locked ward. I was still in the psychiatric unit, but it felt very different. I absolutely didn't feel crazy, and no one was looking funny at me. Dr. Davidson had spoken with Dave McDonald at CHAD, and had gotten much of the story. He agreed that I couldn't be returned to duty there. He arranged for me to meet with the General in charge of all the USAFE medical personnel. The next day I went to Headquarters. The general was just what I would have wanted him to be, tie open and uniform jacket on the back of his chair. We saluted, and I sat down opposite him.

"You don't seem crazy to me. Are you?"

It was my chance to talk where it would count. "No Sir, I have been very unhappy, and I haven't had a chance to be of much use to the Air Force, but I am not crazy." I said this with more assurance than I felt, in the light of the happenings of the past week. Anyway, I was ready to debate. "Then what are all these bad reports I've gotten?"

I tried to give him a concise summary of my total lack of anything to do, my loneliness, and slip in a hint that the colonel might not know what he was doing. I didn't overplay that because the colonel was his man.

"What do you suggest we do?"

"Sir, I would like to be assigned here."

"Well, that's simple enough. I'll talk it over with Dr. Davidson. You can work here temporarily until our second pathologist rotates to the States next month. If things work out, you will be permanently assigned here."

That's the way it was. My diagnosis was changed from *suicidal tendencies* to *acute situational anxiety,* or words to that effect. I was discharged from the Patient Command, attached TDY to the 7100 USAF Hospital, and moved to the Bachelor Officer's Quarters. I became the Officer in Charge of the Pathology section and remained almost a year and a half. The plans for Mary's travel were changed, and she soon joined me. We lived in the Hainerberg officer's housing complex. I was at peace. I did a very good job professionally. We made lasting friends, enjoyed the good life at the officer's club, formerly occupied by Goering and the Luftwaffe elite, and we traveled. It was a wonderful, enriching experience. We even reinforced our German lineage by arranging to have a son born there. So much for the storybook ending.

₧₧

At the completion of my tour, we said deeply felt goodbyes and returned to Camp Kilmer for discharge. As this neared, I became very anxious. I feared the review of my medical history might initiate a delay, further examination and evaluation, even hospitalization, to avoid a possible future claim for service connected disability. Nothing adverse developed, and I was discharged uneventfully. We traveled back to Wisconsin, to present our new son to his grandparents. Before going to the Air Force I had been teaching at Marquette Medical School. I was honored to have been invited by the professor to join him on the faculty of the University of Miami when I returned from service. After a brief vacation, I left Mary with her parents and traveled to Miami. This was an impressive and prestigious opportunity.

The faculty of the newly organized Medical School was an exhibit of valedictorians. Everyone was bright and enthusiastic, with excellent credentials and great promise. It was a powerhouse, like buying the New York Yankees in one deal. I was a natural teacher, with an instinctive sense for which facts and ideas should be spoken in italics. My lectures were a source of pride and reassurance. I was selected by the sophomore class as the teacher of the year. I was additionally pleased that Dr. Anderson was proud of my success. It was an endorsement of his judgement in bringing me with him. He offered me a continuing contract as an associate professor. I gratefully accepted, but in the second year, things were less rosy. The setting and the climate were stranger than life in Germany. Heat and humidity, and mildew and bugs were problems. Mary was lonely. I had occasional feelings of discomfort while I was lecturing, and made sudden awkward adjustments, like turning off the lights and showing slides at unexpected times, sometimes out of context. I instituted a schedule for student lectures, to relieve myself of the tension. Surprisingly, this worked very well. Students preparing their subject for presentation learned more than when they were just passively listening. I divided the class into groups of six or eight for discussions and shared study. I began oral quizzes. This was much less formal, and I wasn't in the spotlight doing all of the talking. If I had a moment of panic, I could just call on a student. The entire class could hear the question, and process an answer, but only one was called on. It was much more interactive learning than the traditional written exam, and very effective. Part of my problem was uncertainty about how I was doing. I was distressed, and often derailed, if I saw a student who was inattentive or doing something other than listening and taking notes. It might indicate that the student didn't like my presentation, or didn't think I was qualified, or I was confused or didn't make sense. I had trouble with questions that sounded critical or contentious.

My personal life presented problems. We moved into an apartment across the street from a member of the Psychiatry department. I became anxious about what he might see or think of my doings. After my Air Force episode I was aware of the possible consequences of anyone giving a bad report about me. I was uncomfortable and afraid. Another neighbor was an old man who stared at Mary when she was wheeling the baby around the block, and in her sense of it, leered and frightened her. I didn't know what I should do. As part of getting our lives in order, I applied for life insurance. The agent filled out the form and I had a routine examination. In time the policy was issued, and I received my copy. As I read it, with an attached carbon of the application, I saw the answer "NO," to the question "Have you ever had any psychiatric illness?" I had lied to the agent. It said at the bottom of the form that false statements would be grounds for cancellation. I was greatly bothered by this, and I wrote to the company, explaining and listing my diagnosis. I received a letter indicating the policy was still in effect, despite the misstatement, but this was a direct reminder of the mess I was in at Chateauroux. These little things kept happening, and I was nervous. I knew someone would find out, and my happy new life would be over.

I began to formulate a rationalized scenario to justify my leaving. I needed the prospect of making more money. To this end, I should take more training in Clinical Pathology, so I could direct a laboratory. Advancement in the academic world was a slow and often politicized process. Even with talent and luck it was a matter of time. Mary wasn't happy. She had little opportunity to meet people and make friends. She didn't like living in Florida. The children should be nearer to the grandparents on both sides. Beneath all of this smoke was the basic fact, I was on the edge of crumbling. Sometime it would leak through, then everyone would know I needed help. All of this was conclusive enough to convince me I should resign. I did it. It startled Dr. Anderson, and no one understood how I could leave. The logic of my arguments wasn't plausible to others, and I had a problem explaining to myself what I was doing. At the completion of the school term we left and returned to Milwaukee.

We stayed with Mary's folks while I searched for a job. I was offered a position at Marquette and also at Mt. Sinai Hospital. I didn't feel able to accept these responsibilities. Very soon I struck on the idea that I would do best in a sheltered position, like a residency. By sheer chance, I was accepted at St. Joseph's Hospital. I must have been a novelty, a resident who was Board Certified. I never inquired of Dr. Altschuler, why he had taken me on, but it was ideal. Training in Clinical Pathology was exactly what I had emphasized in my internal arguments and my public justification. I worked very hard. I was at the hospital before seven o'clock, and I studied most nights until eleven or later. I was rigidly disciplined, never thinking what I was doing; just doing it mechanically, on schedule. I accumulated ring binders full of notes and reprints. I read obscure things like the Proc Soc as we insiders called the Proceedings of the Society for chemistry or experimental esoteric whatever. I learned things no one would think of bothering with. I knew about the Properdin phase of the body's defenses, and the Watson-Crick double helix and the base pairs of guanine-cytosine and adenine-thymidine were everyday conversation topics for me. I studied phenylketonuria and had done chromatographic screening on the retarded youngsters at Southern Colony long before PKU testing of newborns was a statutory requirement. I knew about slow viruses, and the problems that had been perpetuated by the funeral ceremony in New Guinea, of eating the brains of deceased ancestors. I could diagram the formulas of the porphyrins and the cyclopentanoperhydrophenanthrene ring structure. I discussed the transdermal movement of dimethylsulfoxide, discovered in workers in paper mills, thought to be a possible way of eliminating needle injections. I did gradient elution amino acid gas chromatographic studies. The process went on and on, without much direction.

I built a shield of information and trivia to carry me through scrutiny and challenge. Sometimes it worked. I was a quiz kid. I alternately felt superior, intimidating or awkward. This wasn't really therapeutic, but I got some support from it. This ground on for a year. I was just able to keep afloat. We lived in a large older house in Shorewood, owned by John Schmitz, formerly a resident with me at St. Mary's. He carried us, and provided warmth and reassurance. He was the only one who knew my story. At the end of the year, I passed the Clinical Pathology boards. Now, there really was no alternative to going to work.

I was offered a position as an associate pathologist at Waukesha Memorial Hospital. It wasn't much of a hospital, but I thought it would be leisurely, with very little responsibility. I would drift between there and the Medical School, so I accepted. I moved in just before Christmas. The incumbent thought he deserved a vacation, so he took his family to visit the in-laws in Phoenix. The day after he left, I had a frozen section. I was panicked. I had always been part of a group. I would tell a resident to make the sections, and all of us would look at it, discuss it and then give out an answer. I got by. The day after Christmas, the coroner called and asked, in fact, ordered me to perform an autopsy on a women killed while backing out of her drive. She had been struck by a driver in a high speed chase, thrown from her car and then hit by the police in pursuit. I was to determine what and who had caused her death. I presented my findings to a coroner's inquest the following week. This wasn't the low-pressure job I had expected. After New Years, the original Pathologist returned. He was excited about Phoenix, and said he was moving there.

The hospital offered me a contract. I was now the new department head with six employees, and unrelenting anxieties. This was my new base, a temporary safe haven. I hoped to stabilize, and work my way up from there. A few months earlier, while we still lived in Shorewood, my friend John Schmitz, had arranged for me to see Dr. John Stemper, a psychiatrist at the Shorewood Sanitarium. It was essential that I continue this. To fit it in without disrupting my work schedule or attracting attention, I drove to Shorewood every Sunday morning, attended 7 o'clock mass at St. Roberts, then went to the sanitarium. This was very unsettling. Just the word produced a memory of ward 6B. The visits weren't magic, but maybe reassuring. Then I went home, played with the kids, and was more focused than before on what a mess it would make if I faltered. I did eventually change my feeling that this was something shameful, and I was less fearful of being punished. After a year, I was referred to Dr. Saul Pollack, who was conceded to be the best of the traditional psychoanalysts. He accepted me as a patient. I didn't realize then how fortuitous that was. He was expensive and wonderful. I visited him Wednesday afternoons for probably five years. We became very close friends. How I envied the doctors who could play golf on Wednesday.

During these years I sweated and squirmed. Much of the time I was treading water. When I worked on community and church affairs, I hid among the committee workers. I avoided scrutiny. I couldn't risk the prominence of being a president. I was never important, but I must have looked normal. Random, unexpected things came up that flashed me back to Chateauroux. Sometimes there were things I just couldn't do. I had occasional problems in crowds. I didn't feel comfortable in elevators, and I felt the start of panic if the door didn't open immediately. In the early days, when our first interstate highways were built, I didn't use them, because there wasn't an easy way to get off. I drove to Milwaukee on Bluemound. I enjoyed teaching and speaking, but I needed to have a script in hand in case I got flustered and had to read, instead of winging it. I was uncomfortable with people who were intense, or stared at me, especially when I was giving a talk. It was a direct flashback to my early days in Miami. I also discovered I was claustrophobic, when I was to have an MRI. These things changed, and I wore out some of these reactions, or they just went away. Saul said many times it wasn't necessary to find out the causes, just live through the problem, don't act out, and you will forget about it. I believe we agreed that being unaware, unalert, maybe unconscious, was the secret to peace of mind.

I did function effectively most of the time. I survived an attempt to replace me. I developed a school of Medical technology affiliated with Carroll College and the University of Wisconsin. I started the Cancer Registry, and the conferences required for an approved Cancer program. I was fortunate to participate through the years in the ongoing efforts of the hospital to achieve excellence. Our family life was pleasurable and rewarding. We were average, normal and happy. My personal nightmares had faded, and I almost forgot the past. I don't know how much different Mary and the kids might have been if my life were less complicated. I believe they have done well, but I would very much like to have given them a little more self-assurance. I would be thrilled to know that just once someone in our family had been snobbish and patronizing, *cool* in the country club manner. Maybe it would have helped if we were a bit taller.

ℴℴ

Writing these memories has enabled me to identify major currents in the drama of my life. The interacting, often opposing, forces were more readily identified in retrospect. I discovered flaws and weaknesses that weren't evident in the real time of actual living, as I squinted into the hazy future. I was mired in a morass of dreary days without hope or inspiration. The events of Chateauroux overwhelmed me. Uncertainty and loneliness exceeded my tolerance. I have explained away the feelings I carried for the colonel. He may have been only incidental, just the croupier at the gaming table, keeping things moving, but he certainly was heavy handed. I was more vulnerable than I knew, and my infrastructure collapsed. The pragmatic bottom line is I didn't self-destruct. I survived, and surprisingly, no one seemed to know. I am prayerfully thankful for the strength, beyond logic and will, that carried me through. It was a good life at times, but I was never peaceful or secure. This labored explanation has only succeeded in replacing the image of a man with a pile of shards, but I am content with the wisdom of the adage, "We can't know how wonderful the day was, until the night has come."

ℴℴ

Chapter 27

I Shot an Archbishop

I had just returned to Milwaukee from two years overseas as a physician in the Air Force. I was visiting at St. Mary's Hospital, where I had spent three years in residency, renewing acquaintances, and surveying the opportunities for a position. This particular day in the Fall of 1956, in mid-afternoon, I was reading a medical journal and relaxing in the luxury of having no responsibilities, adjusting to the way I thought civilian life should be. A nurse came puffing into the laboratory and announced, "Doctor, Sister Rose would like for you to give the Archbishop a flu shot."

I responded simply, "Nurse, I don't give shots." That was the end of the discussion, I thought. She returned almost before she had left, and more breathless than before, she repeated, "Sister Rose requests you to do this, and she is, after all, the administrator of this hospital."

I knew very well who Sister Rose was. I had endured three years of her Divine Guidance tyranny. She was the original *force to be reckoned with,* but I still said "No, I haven't given a shot for years." The young nurse left again, flushed and flustered, and very certain that her job description didn't say anything about being a messenger.

In a very few minutes, I heard Sister Rose coming down the hall. I knew the distinctive beat of her cane on the terrazzo. When she was agitated it took on an extra syncopation. She, and her assistant, a sweet faced young Daughter of Charity, stood menacingly before me.

As a recent officer and gentleman, and a long conditioned altar boy, I jumped to my feet and almost saluted. "Doctor, I want you to give the Archbishop a flu shot."

I dared to ask, "Why me?"

Her answer was unflattering logic, "You are wearing a white coat, you look the part and you're the only doctor in the hospital."

I demurred. In fact, I refused, but it made no difference. She just stood there. I said, "Sister, you have a troop of nurses who give shots routinely and can do it much better that I. Let them do it."

"No, doctor, the Archbishop must be treated with proper dignity." She turned to the young sister and said, "When He comes, take him to the Emergency Room." She turned abruptly and walked away, with an extra firm tap tap of her cane. She deeply stirred my memories.

The garb of the Daughters of Charity was distinctive, trim folds of royal blue capped by a flaring starched white headdress that had given rise to the whimsical designation God's Little Geese. She wore it with dignity befitting nobility or even a Mother Superior. In the days of my residency she was absolute, a firm medley of sweet and sour. Now, although I was totally free and uncommitted, I still had a conditioned obligation to obey. It may have been the long shadow of my early school days or the more recent stricture of military discipline.

I felt that I had been ordered, commissioned and dismissed in two short minutes, so I waited. Soon the nurse called me to the nearby emergency room where she had taken Archbishop Meyer and his driver and aide, Monsignor Brust. Reluctant and overwhelmed as I was, I entered the room and genuflected in a clumsy undignified manner that said quite eloquently that my heart wasn't in this project. What I managed to say in words was, "Excellency, it is a privilege to meet you." From that moment on, I was in charge, or so it was supposed to be.

The nurse brought syringes and the vial of serum. This was the year Asian flu was discovered, or at least publicized, and everyone was urged to get an immunization. It had received much more attention in the newspapers than it had in the medical literature, so I knew very little about it. Anyway, I rationalized, it wasn't really my concern. I was just trying to readjust to civilian life and find a job. I opened the serum box and scanned the package insert. It identified that this was prepared from duck eggs, and mandated that before it was administered, the patient be questioned about any egg allergy.

Obediently, I asked "Excellency, are you allergic to eggs?"

He answered, "No, I eat them almost every morning."

That was reassuring so I asked the next recommended question, "Do you sleep on a feather pillow?" There were four or five similar insipid questions that didn't seem very penetrating to me, but I asked them, not knowing exactly at what alarming answer I should take corrective action.

The Archbishop interrupted this charade. "Doctor, I sense that you are somewhat reluctant to give me this injection."

That was a considerable understatement. I was totally against it, and I was nervous. I knew almost nothing about the subject, and I didn't give shots. I had been told that Archbishop Meyer was to attend an ordination in Dubuque, and that he should be immunized before he traveled and was exposed to unfamiliar germs. I don't know what higher authority had decreed this, but my immediate orders came from Sister Rose. Even more disturbing, I was told that this was the first dose of Asian flu vaccine that had been released in the Milwaukee community.

I thought that candor was the best approach. "Excellency," I said, "it doesn't matter at all what I think. Considering who you are, you are going to get this shot." Then I turned to the young monsignor, and said "Which of you would like to be first?"

He was a bit flustered. "Of course His Excellency."

I said, "I thought you might want to try it first, like the old time food tasters." My attempt at humor was lost on the Monsignor.

I asked them to remove their cassocks. They did, revealing faded green workaday T-shirts beneath the somber clerical shells, without a distinguishing hint of hierarchical colors, nary a touch of purple. There, standing before me was Archbishop Meyer, soon to be a cardinal, and Monsignor Brust, arms bared, awaiting the ministration of the doctor.

At the moment I was too nervous to appreciate the paradox. These were the guardians of my immortal soul, and I was expected to do some magic to protect their mortal bodies, very much against my wishes.

This was in the good old days before disposable needles and syringes. The nurse drew the proper dose into the syringe and handed it to me. I inspected the needle carefully. It looked good, having been just resharpened the night before. I sponged the Archbishop's arm, pinched a fold of skin and darted the needle into it. The needle bent.

At that moment I would have chosen to be assumed into heaven, or a least to have dropped through a trap-door in the floor. I knew some comment was necessary. "Excellency, it seems we have a rather dull needle here, and we will have to repeat the injection," I mumbled, hoping it would sufficiently excuse me; otherwise, I was dying.

With God-given restraint he answered, "Don't worry, doctor, one has to have a thick skin to be an Archbishop."

I turned to Monsignor Brust and said, "I knew you should have been first."

Chapter 28

Do It by the Numbers

"Man did I get a shock when I heard you were in here. I was in the lounge having a cup of coffee, when someone asked if I knew, and of course I didn't. Tell me what happened."

"It's pretty much the usual story. I guess it isn't anything you expect to happen to you, but when it does, you realize it's about the same for everyone, if they're lucky and make it. I was brought in as an emergency, real 911 excitement. They did a coronary cath, then took me right into surgery. It happened so fast, just a swirl of motion, IV's, drawing blood, shots, tubes stuck in every opening. It must have looked like "*ER*" on TV. I didn't have time to think about anything. In fact, they didn't ask me anything, or even tell me anything. They just did it. The lights went out, and the next thing I knew I was in this room looking for a clock."

"Boy, that's scary, but it is actually reassuring to know that the system really works when you need it. Considering all that commotion you look pretty good. The way things are done these days, I suppose you will be going home in two or three days. I'll stop and see you there; that will be easier than trying to find you here. You wouldn't believe how much time I put in looking for you. I asked a young clerk if you were here in CCU, and she didn't know. After all the time you have spent in this place, and all you have done, she didn't even recognize your name. Incidentally, what do they call you?"

"Jack. That's my name, you know."

"You mean they don't call you *Doctor*?"

"No, I guess that doesn't count for much when you're just a patient."

"How did they register you in admitting? What's on your wrist band?"

"Jack Gordon. Age 70."

"Wouldn't you think the official record should say *Doctor*?"

"Well, my insurance is in the name of Jack and that's what counts."

"Good Lord, don't any of the nurses recognize you?"

"Sure, a few of the older ones do. I took care of their kids They look a little uncomfortable when they hear the young ones giving a report on 'Jack.'"

"Well, I wouldn't like that. You put in thirty years here getting used to that title, and suddenly a young twit decides you're a nobody. It really gets to me. It's part of the whole change of attitude. There's no respect anymore. The newspapers don't print titles, ministers aren't called *Reverend*. Even the President is just a last name. Don't you want to yell at these people and tell them who you are?"

"I don't think that would be a good idea. I remember my dad used to say, 'If you have to tell people who you are, you probably really aren't.' Anyway, I don't want to irritate anyone, You know this process reduces you to infant dependency. You can't eat for yourself. You need help going to the bathroom. You can't get out of bed alone. You very soon get the idea you better behave or they will let you lie there and rot. I don't get a warm feeling that anyone here has ever heard of Florence Nightingale."

"Well, Jack, it may not be perfect, but it sounds like you have it pretty well figured out, and under control. I'll see you at home in a few days."

"Thanks, Bob. I enjoyed the chat. Good luck with the knee

replacement next week. I know things will go well. Remember, we say good luck, but it really is science and skill. Anyway, that sounds convincing. I think I really am proof the system does work. Hey, before you go, just one thing, promise you won't let anyone know you're a doctor or sure enough they'll try to do something different, something nice or special for you, and they'll screw it all up."

Chapter 29

My New Farm

In 1962 I bought a farm. My Iowa grandparents would not have recognized it as such, because their referent for the word "farm" was black loam and straight corn rows. Nonetheless, I acquired title to a piece of land and its contents and inhabitants. This was the culmination of a subliminal yearning germinating from golden moments in my childhood. I was imprinted and driven as inexorably as any salmon making its way upstream. In this quest, I regularly read the classified ads in the Sunday paper at 6 AM, to get ahead of the still sleeping world. It was a vague and uncertain exercise, but I persisted for years. I had established only two criteria: it must be within a two hour driving distance, and it must be reasonably priced, although this was nebulous and elastic.

Routinely I circled the most appealing ads, those that somehow resonated with my ill-defined nostalgia, and then plotted the route for our exploration. The kids were cajoled and coerced into the station wagon, taking them from their friends and their plans for a movie or game or school activity. Off we went on a predictably tiring and disappointing venture. We played all the standard time-wasting games, twenty questions, (you know, animal, vegetable, or mineral) counting cows in the pasture, then losing all of them if we came upon a cemetery on your side, looking for out of state license plates, searching for signs containing the next letter of the alphabet, singing, riddles, and on and on. It was deadly and unfair, and I often resolved to change, but then I rationalized that togetherness was good for all of us.

Inevitably the kids developed more urgent interests and demands. An uprising was imminent. It was signaled by small grumblings, and an irreverent son began to refer to these outings as: *searching for a nursing home*. There wasn't an open rebellion, but a firm resistance developed. I continued in a halfhearted manner, but I don't believe I really expected to find anyplace that could match my memories, and I wouldn't settle for anything less. It was an impasse. I continued reading the ads, but indifferently. We changed our schedule. Wednesday afternoon was the traditional time for doctors to play golf, or in my case, do whatever I chose. Mary was a hapless captive, and submissively accompanied me on my sporadic forays. In all of this floundering, we developed a rich appreciation of our local geography and accumulated a didactic file of nature lore.

Wisconsin is an ecotone created by the convergence of three biomes, the eastern hardwood, the northern conifer forests and the mid-western prairie. This provides a bountiful diversity of animal and plant life. Within it is a geologic formation known as the Kettle Moraine, providing an additional subset of unique features. As the Wisconsin glacier receded, large deposits of transported *foreign* rocks and crushed debris were left at the melting margins. These are the dramatic moraines forming undulating ridges and hills, alternating with deep potholes or kettles. This imaginative topography and diverse biology combine to form a showcase of dioramic displays of both science and beauty.

My resolve was faltering. Then it happened. One Sunday morning, so like the others, I was looking at the ads, resigned to accept what was not to be. Suddenly, there it was. It wasn't pulsating neon, just an inch of print on a whole page of competing offerings, as inconspicuous and as small as a classified could be, yet I knew with frightening certainty that it was different. Because we had discontinued our Sunday family-style excursions months before, I would have to wait until the following Wednesday when Mary and I would go. I called to get directions, and made an appointment. This turned out to be a dreary day, even moreso than the usual for late November. If I had read anything into this as a portent, we would have stayed home and gone to a movie. However, with true Germanic persistence we went. It was an uneventful, dull drive of seventy six miles, well within our defined perimeter limits. We had agreed that we would not spend more time driving to our retreat than we could put in enjoying it. Light mist mixed with snow flurries created a sense of isolation, and we felt detached and unreal. Our first view of the property was disheartening. There was a crumbling cement block building, the size of a garage, at the entrance. A worn, rutted dirt and gravel road opened from the highway and extended back into the unknown. The land was empty, gray and lifeless.

With compass in hand we walked very tentatively, and made our way perhaps five hundred yards from the road. We could not see far because of the haze. The heavy horizon closed us in a world of five acres or less, but as we walked this was ever changing, like leaving one room and entering another. We could recognize a row of low hills arranged in a circular manner around a central low marshy area. It reminded me of volcanic craters I had seen in travelogues. For some reason the Serengeti came to mind, and I thought of wildebeasts. Such was my mental state after years of yearning. There appeared to be a fringe of forest, but it was a smudge without detail, a forbidding wall that posed the ominous question of what lay beyond. We plodded against the weather, uncovering the horizon an acre at a time. It was beginning to snow steadily, and although this was threatening, it softened the harsh and drab into cottony beauty. I thought of Robert Frost's poem *Stopping by Woods on a Snowy Evening*. We, similarly, were engulfed in the silent beauty of winter in the woods. The open ground was rocky, and covered by a shag of dead grasses and protruding weeds that still had distinctive pods and seed heads. Occasional evergreens, lonely and dignified, added color contrast, but they were too sparse to have much effect. A few small animal tracks, and the patient leaf buds on the trees, were the only evidences of life.

We had wandered for about two hours through this kaleidoscope of scenes, broken up and separately framed by the heavy day, but we could not fuse them to gain a sense of what the panoramic composite would be. That would require a clear day with a long horizon. On this day of constricted opportunity, the place felt forlorn, with only spotty promises of beauty. It looked neglected, as indeed it had been. This enhanced its appeal, and added pathos, perhaps like an unwanted, snuffling, tattered orphan. Silent eons pulsed around us, and the rocks gave witness to a past time long before men. On this strange day, as in another world, we had a moment of transcendent peace, sharing with the world's oversoul; yet the little child within us was afraid.

Mary and I were reluctant to admit we liked it. There was too little evidence to judge whether this was the complete answer to our dreams and yearnings. Nothing promised a May carpet of trilliums on the woods floor, or birds flitting through the canopy of awakening leaves. The stinging wind denied it, but we knew we would have to decide, and with no way of getting additional information. We agreed with each other that we should buy it. I would return on another day, and discuss it with the realtor.

My next visit was two weeks later. I went with our second son who was about twelve. We met the realtor in a small sagging house at one corner of the property. He introduced us to the owner, an older man, who just happened to be his father. One leg had been amputated because of diabetes. He had removed his artificial leg so he could sit more comfortably. I had worked my way past enough car salesmen to know that it was a necessary strategy to appear critical and indifferent. I expected a pressure performance from the realtor. He would now emphasize the urgency of my making an offer to counter the existing ones. Not so. The father simply asked if I had seen the land, and if I liked it. I said yes, perhaps too eagerly. I felt I had betrayed myself and lost my bargaining edge. He said it was 132 acres, and how much did I want. I told him I definitely didn't want the old house, but the size of my purchase would depend on the cost. I was stunned when he said the price was eighty three dollars an acre. He agreed that I could mark off the part I didn't want and he would have it surveyed. I signed a paper, indicating I wanted to buy 126 acres, and the ordeal was over. We now had a farm that we had not really seen, but we were confident that we had been guided. This was December 3, the anniversary of my mother's birthday, and the feast day of St. Francis Xavier. What intercessors could have been more ideal than an unorthodox farm girl and a patron saint of foreign lands.

Our next visit together was about two weeks later. We would not have recognized the farm from the fragmented impression we gained on our first stumbling exploration.

It had snowed lightly. Everything was pristine. The sky was cloudless, and the sun glinted from each diamond flake. Everything was transformed, and we could scan the entire land, around the horizon, with one sweep. The marsh crater was a bowl of cream with the rounded hills protruding like dumplings. With the simple beauty of naked lines, the skeletal trees preened against the snow. With the title carefully tucked away at the bank, I no longer read classified ads at 6 AM. We waited impatiently for Spring. The Christmas holiday season had never been so meaningless. January and February droned on interminably. March was probably as ambivalent as usual, but it tweaked and teased us, as we imagined green sprouts where the snow had cleared, and we were frustrated.

These days were like a novitiate, testing us to prove we were worthy of the great things to come. We devoted hours to examining the survey and the aerial maps, and from the topographic map we knew the ups and downs and the steepness of our hills. I even constructed a clay model of the farm, and baked and painted it. We knew the extent of our domain, but a priori, we couldn't know the magic of it before we actually stood there.

By April the snow was mostly gone, and melting rivulets oozed through the mud. Now we began pioneering, exploring and planning. We were breathless, and shared new discoveries of shoots and buds and worms, or a special vista, or tracks with excited shouts. We wanted to see every changing perspective. We were happiest with the sense of our remoteness. It was a delight not to see any neighboring buildings, and we pictured ourselves alone in a primeval world. There was a forest of about forty acres spread over one corner bordering on the marsh. This was of good quality, and we came to the learned stage of glibly referring to it as a mesic climax forest. This was certainly a pretension, but one we enjoyed with simple pleasure. We dredged a large pond in the marsh. It became home to wood ducks, geese and muskrats. We stocked it with bass, but they either froze out or joined the food chain of the raccoons and kingfishers. We graded a road diagonally across the farm to have better access. This was lightly graveled, but after two seasons the weeds and daisies reasserted their claim, and it became again little more than a grassy path. We made other plans to tailor the land to our concept of beauty, but some were inappropriate or didn't fit the personality of the land, and others, like the gravel road, were simply rejected by an uncompromising nature.

Our most successful project was building a house. This was about 500 feet from the county highway, at the edge of the woods.

In the beginning it overlooked the pond, but the next year seeds germinated in the dredged spoilbank, that had last seen the sun during the Devonian era. They flourished and partially hid the pond. Some type of iris was the only flower I could identify. We planted five thousand tree seedlings, mostly spruce and firs, around the perimeter, reinforcing our isolation. As a token, I hand-planted five hundred white pines on a hillside, and learned how sensitive plants can be to nuances of wind and light. They grew only up to a certain line, on the northern slope. It was almost frivolous, but the state gave us five hundred black walnuts, so we planted them. I knew this was the northern range of their tolerance, and every year the saplings froze and new shoots grew from the roots. I liked the learned sound of the Latin names so I posted signs, *Juglans nigra*, and in the case of the pariah box elder, *Acer negundo*. I read of a newly discovered tree growing in China. It was called Dawn Redwood. I ordered one and planted it, reasoning that we were in a similar latitude. This had the lovely and impressive name of *Metasequoia glyptostroboides*. During this period of our planting Grandma Rubert died. We named the tree after her, feeling that such stalwarts deserved each other, Carrie the metasequoia, and Carrie the Iowa farm wife survivor. Unfortunately, the tree was less hardy than grandma, and withstood only one midwest winter. Years later we saw these magnificent trees in the National Arboretum and realized how appropriately we had named ours. On a more self-serving note, we trenched in crowns of asparagus, following the detailed instructions from the book. We anticipated a surfeit of stalks, one of our favorites. Someone shared the local folklore that inasmuch as this originally was a tidewater plant, thriving in briney marshes, the addition of salt would stimulate and enhance its growth. We salted it abundantly, and discovered in a few days that the deer had trampled the plants to extinction, enjoying their private saltlick.

Morels, the queen of mushrooms, little Disney sponges, natives of the Hobbit kingdom, wild and capricious, never cultivated, will of the wisp, here this year and gone the next, grew with abandon securely sheltered in patches of poison ivy. None of the elders had any folk wisdom to explain this. Wild apple trees were randomly scattered around the farm, spread by birds in a more natural way than by a meandering eccentric. One special crab bloomed every other year. We chose its fruit for our experiments developing our private recipe for brandied apples.

Our encounters with wildlife were very special, and sensitive, equally dramatic and tender: the sunset upward spiral of the woodcock's courtship flight and then tumbling seemingly out of control; by rarest chance finding twin fawns motionless in a grassy nest; nearly stepping on drab pebbles strewn on the road, only to realize that the frantic wing dragging antics of the kildeer were an attempt to lure us away from her eggs. Turtles had a favored runway from the pond to nesting sites in the banks. We found curled, tough plastic shells, like used pingpong balls, remnants suggesting a raccoon orgy. Hawks returned annually to their reserved nesting platforms. Sandhill cranes, on the far side of the pond, could be mistaken for shocks of grain, until they moved.

Indirect evidence of animal activity was even more challenging. This had a suspenseful who-done-it quality. Tracks and scats stated emphatically that something had been there, and at the other end of this trail was the something. In one area of scrub alder, we found a prodigious accumulation suggesting there had been a national convention of rabbits. We didn't see woodchucks, but one hill was so undermined it was threatening to walk there for fear of an implosion and collapse. Skunks likewise were furtive, rarely seen, but they left evidence of their activities in the tornup areas they ravaged searching for grubs. With certain animals, tracking is a double game.

It is commonly suspected that foxes double back and watch their pursuers, and although we very rarely saw them, we smelled their presence, slightly less dominating than a skunk, and we knew we were under scrutiny.

With this glut of nature we almost became jaded, and developed a ho-hum attitude. Eventually it did require something special to get our attention. One outstanding experience happened with an owl. I had been dive-bombed by one, and we knew they were present by their evening solos, but they were reclusive. One evening we drove into the yard and were getting out of the car, when we saw this large bird flying from the deck railing into the lawn and then back. This was repeated many times. We sat quietly and watched. We were able to see that it was catching grasshoppers. After fifteen minutes, we decided we had to go into the house. If this disturbed it, then the floor show was over. So be it. Then we paused, wondering if it might attack us. With little alternative we risked it, and ran into the house. From the inside, we were only three feet away, just the other side of the window pane. Eventually, as it darkened, we dared to turn on the porch floodlight. Now we saw the lovely markings of a bard owl, poised for the next sortie into the grass. Then he returned to perch again on the rail with a beakful of grasshopper. Even this dramatic, one of a kind, exhibition grew monotonous. I had never been this close to a wild bird before, certainly not a raptor. It became as routine as watching finches at a window feeder. I wanted to go the next step. I called a friend who was a professor of Biology to ask what would happen if I gently walked out and tried to stroke it, or perhaps offer my arm as falconers do in the movies. No answer. We decided not to interrupt the banquet, so we went casually on with our supper and TV. When we went to bed two or three hours later, the carnage was still going on. Sometime later I asked the professor what would have happened had I done what I proposed. Would we have acquired a pet? He destroyed my Dr. Doolittle illusions, saying I probably would have made a trip to the ER for sutures.

Our hours in the woods were spiritual. The messages were whispers without words. Wisdom and beauty suffused directly, unfettered by ideas or knowledge. This aura of softness and wonder required none of our senses. In Spring the forest floor was blanketed white, not with snow, but thousands of trilliums. Our most precious find was a cluster of six giant yellow ladyslippers. Each year we located them, reassured that the force governing such things was still in control. We thought of trying to transplant them to a more accessible spot, where we could enjoy them more readily and provide protection. However, we conceded we could not improve on the present success. We caressed the sensuous pillars of the beech trees, long before it was politically sound to hug trees in your campaign speeches. We meditated on lichens and shelf fungi, appreciating the wonder of simple things, and we listened for the harmonious silence of the muted orchestras of nature.

In the evenings we read the Title Abstract of the past hundred years, and tried to experience life in that world. This read like a Greek tragedy. It was a cavalcade of despair, as a succession of settlers, with fresh hope, tried to force a living from the unyielding rocks. As if foredoomed and predictable, they faltered. Then, cramped and starved, in final defeat, they filed a quit-claim deed and moved with only a wagonload of their meager possessions. We read of two dozen or more dreams, broken in this unequal contest with the earth, before we came, and were adopted. We felt compassion, but also fleeting guilt for our pleasure. We realized that this was simply a matter of different expectations. We came in peace, not to conquer the land, and we asked for little but poetry. I often wondered what my grandparents would have thought. There was little similarity between the two so-called farms, one with rocks and trees and the other exuding fertility, but my grandparents also had dreams and soul. Sometimes, to the detriment of their fullest use of the land as a productive resource, they planted flowers instead of crops. In reverie, I slip the limits of time, and meld the flatland farm of my youth in perfect union with the hills and ponds of the present. I know they have forgiven my presumptions.

We now had title to the farm. There is a deep satisfaction in this, even if one knows and accepts the concept that it is not possible to *own* anything. I chose deliberately to call this our *land.* It sounded respectful, not just utilitarian. It allowed for mystery and unknown wonders, not just a destination defined by fences and plowed rows. I accepted the responsibility for protecting this, in the Biblical sense of stewardship. We assumed we had the right to sculpt it slightly, and bend it to our use. We built a cottage, dredged a pond, planted trees, anchored erosive forces and planted browse for the deer. It was many idealized things, a home, a learning center, a laboratory and a cathedral. It was a refuge, and the most real material element in our lives. We wanted to sort out the trivial and live with the essence, very much what I thought Thoreau would have done. These experiences, and these values, pervaded our family and today are the core of our being. One couplet expresses it all: "One impulse from the vernal wood may teach you more of man, of moral evil and of good, than all the sages can."

Chapter 30

Continuum

Last sweet autumn days,
Soft beyond their time.
Faded memory of youthful green,
Gossamer hint of pastel perfume,
Faint echoes of warbled song,
Drying sediment of summer.
Dream suspended in delay
Pierced by errant darts
Of sudden winter chill.

With slant graying of the light
Comes a lullaby of snow,
To soothe the forlorn crinkley earth.

Guardian pines abreast
In staunch array resist,
That gentler life below
May rest and be reborn.

Chapter 31

Resignation

It was Friday, the last day of the workshop, when I was scheduled to read. I thought about this, and didn't understand. Why was I the last one? Was I the best, saved for the last? In simple reality, I knew this was unlikely. Perhaps it was in deference to my seniority, although throughout the week I hadn't noticed any special respect. I was occasionally aware that I was a bit older than the others, but only when they pushed me out of the way. Was it the seating arrangement, or where my name was in the alphabet? I recalled that there was an almost universal reaction of disaster victims, cancer patients for instance, who cry out, "Why me?" It seems that no one was listening, and as the youngsters say, "I didn't have a clue." Actually that wasn't quite true. I did have a hint, a subliminal glimmer of insight, that perhaps there wasn't enough time to get everyone in, and I was the most expendable. That is to say, the one whose contribution would be missed the least. That certainly was unflattering, even paranoid, and I rejected it, but no other reason really fit, so I floundered on.

I was spared further anguish. Everyone else had finished, and there were still four hours remaining. Whatever the reason, it was now inescapably my turn. My pulse accelerated, and I became sweaty and flustered. I had read enough about panic attacks to know what was happening. I dredged up the advice I had read that was given to people who were afraid of public speaking, "Imagine everyone in the audience is naked." I tried that for just a moment; it was too scary. I told myself that they were human beings, just like me. It didn't help. This was big time, the prestigious, even renowned, University of Iowa Summer Writer's Festival. I must have gone on automatic pilot, because my next recollection was of standing at the lectern, having just pronounced the last period. I knew it was a wonderful story, just a postage stamp away from being published in the New Yorker. I paused, perhaps subliminally expecting applause. There was none. I sat down ready for comments. How could they find anything to correct or improve? I assumed there would be some criticism, but mostly praise and enthusiasm. I knew the workshop procedure. I had participated in it all week. The first round comments must be positive and constructive, at least not critical. Sometimes, in the eagerness to attack, it was difficult to offer something benign, but still meaningful. I sensed they were just treading water. The most penetrating comments were, "You used good bond," and "Only one typo," and "The margins look good, nice and even." This was ominous, all about looks, and nothing about substance, and this was only the mandatory *be nice* phase. Then they rubbed their collective hands, and opened up their true selves.

As they strained forward in the starting blocks, a comment from Flannery O'Connor flashed across my mind, something like, "Beginning writers are self-centered, ignorant and mean-spirited." It wasn't an exact quote, just the essence, but close enough to my situation to make me wish I was someplace else. Then things took off, and the next two hours were light years, instead of the standard one hundred twenty minutes. I began getting repeated rumblings and contractions that said if things got much worse, I would be in the men's room, and it wouldn't be a psychological excuse.

The comments were delivered in such assured, solemn, even dreary voices. Obviously they were advanced and established writers, otherwise how could they be so certain. How had they learned so much?

"Your so-called story was contrived."

"You didn't maintain a consistent voice and point of view."

"Your use of metaphors was excessive, and usually trite."

"As a first person narrator, you couldn't know all the things you described."

"There were too many characters. They were cardboard and not fully developed."

"There was no central conflict. No tension. The protagonist was unchanged."

"Your words were too flowery, and it was overwritten."

This is just a partial list. When I later reviewed all the critiques, I thought it would be an excellent outline on how not to write. Worst of all, under the rules of the workshop, I wasn't permitted to answer or explain, until all the comments were completed. By that time I had forgotten most of them, and I was overwhelmed by the total futility of it. This wasn't a debate, and I was expected to be appreciative of such a high level learning opportunity, and not bicker, so I didn't. I gathered up my shredded dignity and escaped without whimpering. I was only an apprentice writer who paid big money for the benefits of constructive mutilation.

I limped back to the Holiday Inn, and soaked in hot water and self pity. In a few days I had recovered enough to try to retrieve some fragments of ego, so I sent my story to the New Yorker. I would be vindicated, and show these experts. The expected interval between submission and getting a check averaged three months, according to the Writer's Digest. In exactly nine days my manuscript was returned with a sterile rejection slip. I was troubled by the short time required to decide to reject it, but even more so by the fact that the paper clip didn't appear to have been removed. It suggested that judgment was made from the first page. I had to work up an excuse or explanation to soothe my damaged ego. I knew in my heart it was the result of the shoddy standards of the new editor, Tina Brown. She knew nothing about good fiction, and favored vulgar, sexy trash. I predicted she would run the New Yorker into failure.

I haven't fully regained my confident self image, and no one has yet sullied my pristine unpublished status. I haven't conceded, but I have accepted the possibility of some limitations, and have settled into a functioning, comfortable niche. I attend writing courses, but I don't expect miracles, certainly not from some of these instructors. One of my idols, Paul Gallico, said when invited to teach a class at Columbia University, that he didn't think he could teach anyone to write, but he could guarantee to do no harm.

I am enjoying my non-competitive life, with no goals or aspirations. In my peer group of amateurs, I am continually surprised at the diversity and richness of talent. I listen to the crispness of their recall, the sensitivity of their memories of long ago events, the fresh flavor and poetry or their word choices, and the drama emerging from each epiphany. I have seen blue-haired grandmothers dance from the page in saddle shoes and bobby sox, teasing and flaunting in their over-stuffed angora sweaters. The men, recast as awkward Brilliantined boys, with menacing pimples, suffer the delicious anguish of fighting to suppress impure thoughts. I compare these earnest aspirants with the jaded and arrogant posturing of the self important groups I have known.

I recall the exchange between Oscar Wilde and George Bernard Shaw as they discussed an especially clever comment by one of their friends. Reportedly, Oscar said, "I wish I had said that," to which Shaw replied, "You will, Oscar, you will."

With this endorsement of plagiarism, I make careful notes of the best images, the most vivid metaphors, and the best phrases, and I file them. I am grateful for this hors d'oeuvre sampling of many vintage lives. Someday, when my folder is filled, I will mix them together and publish my own masterwork. I will certainly take all credit, but the criticisms, if there are any, will be widely distributed, and the parentage dispersed.

ೞೞ

Healing

After my bruising encounter with the learned at the writing school, I continued to plod, untaught, trying by clumsy effort to express myself. I concentrated on the simplest form, writing my life story. I already knew the characters and the plot. I only had to master the juggling of words, selecting those most appropriate for telling my story in a convincing and sympathetic way. I sometimes have had difficulty maintaining balance between the thoughts and the rigidity of translating them into words. I am the narrator, an intermediary, recalling and telling. I am an archivist, but not a slavish historian. I may embellish and flavor to enhance my pleasure, and perhaps hold a stray reader. I am an essayist who editorializes, injecting opinions and forcing conclusions. I try not to overdo any of these, but really it is my story as I choose to remember it. If I fabricate, or wander from the strict truth, I am soothed by the wisdom that "Consistency is the hobgoblin of little minds." Some writers refer to this exercise as reinventing the past.

The question of why one bothers to write at all, eventually has to be dealt with. It is a compelling force within me, so deep it may even be gene-linked. Writing helps to anchor and confine those wispy dollops, formless without words, that merely graze in the back-pasture of my mind. My best efforts to understand yield specious answers. I do know with certainty that I write because it is a private way for a little man to react to the things in the world he can't control. It also is my voice to sing of all the beauty and wonders without a concern about being off key. It is the freedom to solve world problems without testing the results. I write to extend myself beyond my natural life span, and though I dislike intruding, I dream vaguely that sometime a distant great-grandchild may read it, and wish he could have known me. This is the ultimate vanity. Most immediately, and personally, I write because it is a shield against loneliness.

Chapter 32

The Out of Town Expert

I was frantically trying to say, "No," while his good-bye words were still tingling along the wire. What had he really said?

It started with, "I'll take you to lunch at the club when you are in Hilton Head." Before I could get excited, he added, This will be something of a quid pro quo deal."

The polite Latin talk translated as *watch out,* so I asked defensively, "What does that really mean?"

I Ie changed the subject with, "It will be good to see you."

I persisted. "What's the trade off?"

"Oh, nothing really, we have this little writing group here. We call ourselves The Nostalgics. We have been discussing ways in which we might improve our writing, something of a critique. Actually, we call it an evaluation; that sounds more peaceful. In this light I happened to mention you, and suggested to the group that you might be willing to share with us some of the magic from the Iowa Summer Writing Festival."

That completely destroyed my excitement and my appetite for lunch. No one in his right mind would want to cruise into a closed group and try to sound like an authority. My reflex inclination was to shout, "No way," but as I stuttered and mumbled, he said, "See you in two weeks," and hung up.

As I was looking for the number to dial back, I ran the idea from the left to the right brain, and back again. It sounded a bit better when I said it out loud, and I felt positively good. I liked the upbeat ring of, "I have been invited to address a prestigious writers' group at Hilton Head Island." My flimsy pedigree would certainly be enhanced if I played this up.

So, essentially by chance or serendipity, it was decided. I was going to be there anyway, and what did I have to lose. They might just be nice people. Fat chance. I replayed some of the scenes from the Iowa adventure, and I factored in the vaguely remembered comment I attributed to Flannery O'Connor, that beginning writers were self serving, mean spirited and a few other choice qualities to that effect. Nonetheless, I processed and rehearsed a few basic ideas. I dredged up a bushel of notes, and pearls from my wanderings. I had saddle sores from being bucked around during the workshops, but perhaps I could actually say something helpful. I worked up a lecture, prepared a handout of precepts, dogmas and an inspiring quote from E.B. White, made fifteen copies and tucked them carefully into my most professorial appearing briefcase. I now was ready for a dazzling half hour presentation. I thought no more about it, but as the world turns, the day inevitably arrived.

My friendly sponsor picked me up at the parking area, and we drove importantly past the guard at the front gate, up to the sanctum of the Hilton Head Plantation Club House. As we walked up the curving staircase, my friend said, "Oh, by the way..." Few expressions in civilized exchange convey more of a warning. I had a primitive alert response, ready for flight. The hairs on the back of my neck sprung up as he continued, "...this writers' group is quite formally structured. There are officers and committees and all those business things. I think there is even a treasurer."

I was intrigued; I had never seen a creative writing CEO. We opened the door and fifteen curious faces, positioned around a thirty foot board-meeting table, turned toward us as if we were intruders.

The presiding voice said "We have just completed the minutes and treasurer's report. Is there any old business? I welcome you. You arrived just at the proper moment."

Whether by chance, or by prearrangement we were ten minutes past the designated starting time. I interpreted this as allowing time for the members to settle in and ready themselves for the next order of Business: *Me*. The chairman motioned us to the only empty chairs, and we sat. One of the benign faces spoke next. Perhaps he sensed that a touch of human nature should be on the agenda.

"We have been discussing how best to fit invited guests into our meetings. If we have them as the first item of business, it will reduce the time that remains for each of us to read what we have prepared. That is contrary to our main purpose. If we put them on at the end, there may not be enough time for them to make their presentation. Should we just set a limit of twenty minutes and let it go at that?"

A few comments followed. Someone suggested that there only be visitors two or three times a year. I thought they might have forgotten that I was an invited guest. I interpreted this as a tribute to how easily I fitted in, and they were sharing their problem with me. One solution was to start the meetings earlier. Being the source of the problem, I felt uncomfortably qualified to make a suggestion. Why not just go around the table in the usual random order, and I would talk when it came my turn. That was a bit inexact and simplistic, and it didn't really solve such a knotty issue, but it got things moving, and anyway it was only a trial.

They began reading in succession, counterclockwise. This was a shrewd move, it put me in the middle. When my turn came the chairman said, "Bob, if you don't mind, we will skip you, so as to allow you uninterrupted time at the end."

Increasingly I wondered what I was doing there, possibly my friend had not checked it out with the program chairman. As they say in polite circles, I acquiesced gracefully, and cooperatively said that was very thoughtful. In the following hour of captivity, I shared gentle memories of a beloved aunt, a 1400 mile bike tour of France, a whimsical account of a man's face lift, a painful adventure of a college professor as a substitute high school teacher, a charming, very English reminiscence, a moment of dewy poetry and a wistful cameo of young love.

After such an eclectic smorgasbord, I felt totally anticlimactic. What I had planned to say was redundant if not irrelevant. I shifted into free flight.

"I came here to explore with you the methods and benefits of critiquing your writings. Presumably this would improve their quality. I have listened to your readings. They are warm and intimate, and present a rich diversity of experience and feeling. You are sensitive, and share deep concerns. You provide each other a gentle, receptive sounding board for your memories. I would caution against changing any of that. Forced evaluation or criticism can create tensions that will destroy the magic of your spontaneity and trust. You are not writing primarily to be published, and do not need approval. Perhaps you are taking a small step toward immortality, hoping to present yourself to a future generation as a real person with flavorful, distinctive qualities. I came with a didactic message and formulary handouts, but you don't need them. Don't concern yourselves with arbitrary standards, or the current fads in writing. You already have the skills to recreate your memories."

I folded my handouts, stuffed them into the briefcase, shook hands, accepted thanks, and moved on with my friend to collect the promised free lunch. I am not a big lunch type, so I settled for a cup of soup, but I did steal a few fancy cocktail napkins to prove I had really been at Hilton Head.

Chapter 33

December 14, 1988 — Today We Sold the Farm

You know that this unwanted conclusion has evolved simply as a product of passing time. Our lives were changing and diverging, and it was no longer possible for any of us to use the farm as we once did. We will cherish the warm memories of little people playing around the oak table, building a tree house, eating at the Schwarz, watching wildlife and discovering the little miracles of nature.

Unfortunately, this is no longer possible. In recent years mother and I have gone to the farm with excitement and anticipation, but have returned home a few hours later with the glum realization that it was empty; there was none of the warmth and meaning that we, as a family, had put into it.

Reluctantly, we were forced to accept the conclusion that the farm of memory was wonderful, but the present reality is only a depressing reminder. We see trees we planted, the pond we dredged and the paths we made as we imprinted the farm to our use. All of this is past. We are no longer putting any creative new thought into it. We are not enhancing it, and it is not enriching us. Because we could not find a better way, we drifted to the decision we should sell.

This has been a grinding process, dominating us waking and sleeping. We have had appraisals, surveys, legal and tax consultations, rezoning hearings, furniture sales, moving aches and finally, a closing.

On our last visit we only stayed an hour, then we drove through the gate, stopped, put the chain on and padlocked it. We started to drive away, then stopped again, thinking perhaps something might have changed and this wasn't really happening. We got out of the car and stood without speaking, as we gazed vacantly down the gravel road for a last look at the cottage. I thought of Robert Frost. Only one road.

This has affected me deeply. I identify with depression farmers who were forced from their farms, and with Grandma Rubert who anguished over the sale of their farm after Grandpa died. Our sale is heavily layered with these residuals. For an Iowa boy with a farm in his genes, it is a chilling feeling to be stripped of his most basic possession.

Perhaps we have simplified our lives, and are now open to new experiences. But, why do we now feel contracted and poorer? The only last line possible in this lament is that time brings inexorable changes without concern for better or worse.

Chapter 34

Rationalized

Not long ago I was reading some of the poems of AE Hausman. One of them was the sweet, nostalgic, "When I was one and twenty, I heard a wise man say." I have certainly heard wise men, but sometimes I didn't listen. Now with the polarity reversed, I am in the position that I should be making the wise pronouncements. Unfortunately, I am having a bit of difficulty with my self-image, and getting through to my intended youthful audience. This forces me to a definition of youth. Intuitively, I tend to concede that it is anyone who is younger than I. Of course, I know it isn't just years, but this is like debating how big is big. Regardless of semantics, I know what the reality is.

I remember vividly the time when I first became old. It wasn't a specific event or a single day. Nothing extra dramatic happened. It wasn't a seismic disturbance. It was cumulative, an aggregate of little things in synergistic combinations. I can't even identify most of these factors. I don't think I suddenly began acting old. I didn't change my behavior or activity pattern much. I doubt if most people noticed the difference, but it was a moment of inescapable epiphany. I finally accepted that the world, and life with a capital L, had changed around me, and that I couldn't adjust spontaneously, in a simple rebalancing way. Accommodation was no longer a reflex. It required labored, often painful, rationalizing to justify my being. I was out of step, and I knew I was old.

For some time these nagging feelings of discomfort, even resentment, have been lurking just beneath the surface, threatening to break through into my consciousness. Much more than a visible change in me, is the gap that youth has opened between us. Quite abruptly they seem different, focused on themselves, overwhelmingly sure, and always on their cell phone. Of course, it is Biblical for elders to bemoan the ways of the young. Scripture advises, "If you think the present generation is worse than the former, you have not inquired wisely." Mine is not a judgment; it is an envious regret that I no longer fit in, or have much relevance. It required an avalanche of festering evidence to force this conclusion on me.

My hair is thin, and what remains is white. My skin is wrinkled, and sags. My vision and hearing are declining. My body is less erect. I move more slowly. I have less endurance and strength. These are the externals that indicate I am entering the common pool of aging. Gone are those distinguishing qualities that set each of us apart as individuals: beautiful, lithe, athletic, graceful, talented, forceful, brilliant and charming. With these replaced by their ugly opposites, aging is so painfully evident, but incredibly I never felt this inventory checklist applied to me. I saw such changes jarringly displayed in my friends, who pretended to be unaware of how damaged they were.

My blithe self-image had to be bolstered by energetic denial, and required continuous maintenance. I have reams of paper that attest to my accomplishments, and my worth. In spite of all this comforting support, aging came upon me insidiously, not as a cognitive loss or physical faltering, but as a decline in the instinctive assuredness that is the essence of maturity. Inescapably, I was forced to admit that I had changed. My ambience is no longer grand, and I do not think in graceful iambic rhythm. I am mundane, and I am almost content just to be so. I am habituated to a secure routine, the same route to the store, to the church, to a restaurant. I expect to see the same people, who also expect to see me. I have a standardized speech pattern. My greeting is "How are things in your world?" I am not experimental. I am not adventuresome. I am less creative. I thrive on predictability. Worst of all, the offspring treat me with gentle tolerance, patronizingly patting me on the head. I fear they find me archaic and boring.

E.B. White wrote with eloquent simplicity of a childhood vacation, and shares the nostalgic confusion of a later trip revisiting the lake, hand in hand, with his son. "I began to sustain the illusion that he was I, and therefore, by simple transposition, I was my father. This sensation persisted. I seemed to be living a dual existence."

I have experienced similar nuances in quiet and unguarded moments. I find myself without clear focus, and on a mystic ground where the real present and the flavored past blend inseparably. As we talk and share, in a figurative way, I feel the same question. Although I no longer speak the language of youth, nor they mine, I treasure these melded dream bonds that bridge between us, more than my own reality.

Chapter 35

Beyond Value

It was Friday, August 12, 1994. The three of us were sitting in this upscale restaurant, someplace between the Drake and the Water Tower. It was dark, either restful or provocative, depending on your mood. Each of us had a different reason for being there. I was carrying my mother's old violin and had come to Chicago to have it appraised. My wife was with me. She shared my curiosity about its value, and she was happy just to see the glittering good life of the Windy City, and maybe buy a trinket or two. The third was a friend who came for the food. He was willing to drive to Chicago just for lobster ravioli. This was complete nonsense to my way of thinking, but since I didn't especially like driving there, it was a good arrangement. We settled into a glass of wine. Of course, it had to be a *Chard* because we were having lobster, even though it would be mutilated beyond recognition. We went through the ritual of discussing how much oakiness was needed, and ultimately bowed to the recommendation of the sommelier. I don't really like chardonnay, and would have preferred a beer, but the ambience pressured me to try to be genteel. The oh so smooth lunch crowd annoyed me. I thought they were all frauds, trying to impress each other, and probably with overdue credit card debts. It was something like a latter day Noel Coward thing, "Oh, dahling, you look ravishing," and all that. I was just plain uncomfortable. It was a high round table with tall stools, intended to suit the beautiful people on the go, who couldn't spare the time to sit down and relax. It also served to show off lots of leg, if you were inclined to notice. My wife didn't seem to mind, and our driver just perched there in his stolid way, as if daring them to serve something that would excite his jaded taste. He fancied this was the kind of place where he really belonged. It wasn't my choice of the ideal ingredients for an enjoyable lunch.

The food came, in very small servings, and we swirled our wine and commented on its nose. We gulped when the bill came, and we left. The first phase of our adventure was completed, and one of our members had fulfilled his mission. I had no clue as to whether he judged it worth the trip. From past experience, I knew he looked just as dour whether he enjoyed it or not. We had parked in a ramp, so it seemed sensible to take the bus about ten or twelve blocks to our appointment. I had the violin. It was awkward because the old case had lost its handle, and I pretty much had to clutch it with both hands. More than that, it was probably fifty years old, and the leather had worn so it was dry and powdery. Every time I shifted it a bit or rested it on my shoulder, I got a smudge of brown powder on my coat. By the time we got off the bus I was a two toned mess.

I had called weeks before and made an appointment with a renowned company that specialized in rare violins. I was able to give enough vague information to get the appointment. After all, that's the way many of the Cremona masterpieces have surfaced, and every dealer must have a dream of finding a rarity. The address was just slightly south of the Art Museum, on the opposite side of the street, almost next door to the Symphony Hall. We got off the bus and immediately knew this would have to be the place. It looked grand and historic, a proper setting for discovering fine things. From the front it looked like an architectural exhibit, carved pillars of marble and a dramatic frieze which I didn't have time to interpret. The main floor was spacious and empty, but there was an atrium that extended upward through ten or fifteen floors, and in its center was an elevator. There was an old decorative open iron mesh shaft, with the cage elevator moving slowly up and down for all to see. It was manned by a uniformed elderly gentleman, who controlled the operation with a circular lever, announced the floors with an authoritative tone, and closed and opened the folding brass gate with ceremonial dignity. It had much of the lost importance we used to feel about street cars. It was strikingly different from the rapid transit in the skyscrapers. It fit our purpose and mood perfectly. From the first floor we could hear music, and also the discordant squawking and scratching of beginning hopefuls. It was completely in accord with the entire setting. We got off at the fifth floor, and found the offices of Bein and Fushi. We were greeted with some recognition since we had an appointment, and were asked to be seated. At this point I relaxed enough to feel a bit odd. What was I really doing here with an old violin? Had I perhaps misrepresented things that somehow justified our intrusion into this museum level of expertise? In this uncertain and apprehensive mood, I thought back fifty years on what I knew about the violin.

It had been the lifelong ikon of our family's mythology. My mother told me on repeated occasions that her father bought a fine violin for her when she was fourteen. She took lessons from a Professor Crawford. She pronounced his name with reverence, so I knew the professor was a man of substance. She would get out the violin at odd times, usually when she was especially troubled or depressed. It was a bridge for her to better times. She might just examine the instrument, wipe it gently and put it away, or she might begin to play. This had an interesting effect on her. She straightened up to full five foot two, tucked her hanky under her chin, looked ahead into space as if she were on stage and began to play. She didn't play long, and she never played anything I knew. I really didn't like the sound of her music, it seemed very quivery. I know now that this was a calculated tremolo, but I always got a little nervous, and thought she was missing notes. I was happy she never did this when any of my friends were there. This seemed to make her dreamy and thoughtful, and I sensed she was again age fourteen, but soon she was back to normal. She told me that she was quite good, but I had no way of knowing that. Once she showed me that she was fingering near the middle of the strings, and she said this was the sixth position, and it was hard to do. It sounded squeaky to me. I don't think I was very appreciative.

On the positive side, my dad played the violin in a very different style. He played barn dance music. It was called a hoe-down, and when he was sawing away, it was called a fiddle. I liked that, and I could jump around and sing crazy words to Turkey in the Straw and Pop Goes the Weasel. It didn't make much sense, but everyone felt good, and that was pretty rare in our house. I don't know how he learned to do this. He never said much except he "just picked it up." He was the entertainer, and loved to play for hours whenever anyone wanted to dance. Mother's cousin, Lucy, was an old maid who played chords on the piano, repeating and repeating, almost like a drum beat. The two of them were quite a team, much in demand for local shindigs.

It was the same violin they shared, but there was such a difference in the feeling. Even though I liked my dad's jerky stuff better, I had a deeper, sort of sad feeling when mother played. She looked far away, inside herself, and I thought she might be crying. She also was a very energetic dancer. She had a tambourine, and she would get going and kick up in the air, and she could actually slap her hands around and behind her outstretched leg. This embarrassed me, but most folks thought she was cute. One of the most fun times I ever had was when we got snowbound at some farmer's big house and had to stay for two nights. This had started out as just an evening of fiddle and piano music, but it snowed so hard that when it was time to go home, the model T couldn't move. They just kept playing and eating.

I pumped the player piano, roll after roll, and I got to play pool for the first time. All of this happened before my dad got sick and died. After that mother put the violin away. She only played it a few times, just exercises and scales like a student would. I know it reminded her of days past.

I asked her about the crack in the back of the violin one time when she had it out. She didn't know when this had developed or how it came to be. Nothing special had happened to break it. Then she told me they had taken it to a man who built and repaired violins. His name was Nelson or Neilsen and he was a barber. That seemed strange to me, but I guess it was because he was good with his hands. She told me that when he took it apart he had found a small piece of paper glued to the inside. This gave a date, 1756, and a German sounding name, David Christian Haverman. That was very exciting. Years later, after she died and I had it in my keeping, I got curious. I tried to shine a light inside it and read with a small angled dental mirror what was written on the paper. I couldn't make out anything. Another time I took it to a friend who played in the Waukesha Symphony. He put on a couple of new strings, tuned it and played for me. He said it had a good tone, maybe not great, but good. Then I took it to a music store in Milwaukee he had suggested. They fooled with it a bit, but finally said it was beyond their knowledge. They said there was a paper in it, but they couldn't read it any better than I could. They gave me the name of the company where we now were sitting waiting. Inevitably, I got worked up after each of these examinations and I thought maybe mother's violin was really something.

We were taken into an office and I placed the case on the table. A gentleman came in, spread a piece of wine colored velvet on the table, removed the violin from the case and laid it delicately on the cloth. This was the respect given to a masterwork, and I was nervous. He wore a simple business suit, but somehow he had the aura of a celluloid collar and pince nez. His total presence had a sense of class. First he examined the bow which was clipped inside the cover of the case. It seemed he took a long time with it. I didn't know what this had to do with anything, because like the case, it had been purchased separately by her father. I think I was getting impatient. This had been a long time developing, with lots of little hints and clues, false starts, and I just wanted to get it over with. This felt something like going to a doctor. He made a soft "hmm" two or three times, then looked across his finger tips at me, like they do just as they announce you have cancer, and then relaxed a bit. He turned the violin over.

His first understandable words were, "Oh, too bad, it has a crack."

I knew that, but I thought it had been repaired. Then he started talking, and I didn't know if it was for good or bad.

"This is a three-quarter size, obviously made for a young person. The neck and scroll are slightly thicker than usual. The carving isn't as delicate as the Italians. Yes, I think it is consistent with German craftsmanship. You said it has a date and a German name inside. We will examine that later, but you know it isn't uncommon for someone to put a false name and date to mislead a buyer. This isn't necessarily genuine. We see some pretty poor imitations with Stradivarius labels in them. Now this varnish isn't as hard as I would expect. It may have suffered from being polished badly. When I first opened the case, I allowed myself a flutter of excitement. Now, I am not sure. I think if I were to give you an estimate of its value, I would have to say, ah, about..."

I surprised myself and interrupted him. "I don't want you to tell me that. I've changed my mind."

With just common sense, I knew it wasn't a great rarity, and the value for me wasn't the illustrious name of the craftsman, or the long dried wood, or a secret ingredient in the varnish. An estimate in currency terms totally missed the memories of tears and dancing, and the hint of mystery and wonder that had surrounded it through my childhood.

I closed the case and asked what his fee was. With a slight bow and unruffled dignity, he said there was no charge. It was as if, without words, he somehow understood. I thanked him.

This sudden change startled my wife. Our third party thought I was crazy. It had been our principal reason for doing all this. We left the building to return to the car. He didn't speak, just grunted and took off. I had assumed we would take a cab since it was about a mile. I didn't know exactly where we had parked. Mary and I almost ran. I was having trouble carrying the violin, more than I did when we rode the bus. At street crossings we could catch up if the lights cooperated. It was frantic, but we were afraid we might be left behind if we didn't keep up. The cause of this behavior was puzzling. We didn't know if he was embarrassed or disappointed. We had a fleeting view of the exhibit along the mall of Botero bronzes, and would have enjoyed a more leisurely pace, but it wasn't possible.

We finally made it to the car. When we were in and driving north along the Outer Drive, the tone and atmosphere were as congenial as if nothing unusual had happened. It was as if some metabolic or chemical switch had flipped. He announced that we were in for a treat. We were going to have dinner at Froggy's, a little French café he had discovered and wanted to revisit. It was a long day, two absurd pretentious meals, and an unwelcome challenging trip through my memories.

I put the little violin back on the closet shelf, where it awaits any youngster who wants to take lessons, or for one who might pursue its romantic history, although I concede most of this probably is only reverie in the dusty recesses of my mind.

Chapter 36

The Magic Carpet

When I was young I collected stamps. I don't recall when this began. Someone gave me a small album that contained a few stamps scattered through the pages. There was a predominance of empty spaces, but there also were pictures of stamps. On the first page of each country, arranged in alphabetical order, was the flag, a map, the unit of currency, the capital city and sometimes the population. This was my first geography book, a year or two before I got the big one in fifth grade.

The impact this had in those simple days, before the overpowering instant information of TV, is impossible to describe to a young person in today's world. I was teased by little peeks at the distant world. There was the silent cascade of Victoria Falls. Serene leopards, inscrutable gorillas and odd birds, beautiful and ugly, paraded through my world. In TV or the movies, this serene tranquility would be lost, as Marlin Perkins or John Wayne stampeded the wildlife in a jeep. Opulent flowers wafted perfume from the fertile pages. I learned the faces of the famous and the mighty. There were statesmen and tribal rulers in official dress. The maps showed how the world would look if it were possible to view it from an all encompassing height, and they displayed the jumble man had made by subdividing it. The nations and alliances, the majesty of great empires, the spectacle of coronations, a native king crowned under an arching bower of elephant tusks, all were there. Even little countries had a page. They were often more alluring than the giants, in their misty remoteness. Ideas and inventions were exhibited. Great achievements were commemorated. I travelled from the silk and spice roads of Marco Polo to the mills and factories of European industry, from tribal carpets to Brussels laces. I flitted from kabuki to Caruso at the Met. Art was everywhere, the Louvre, the Hermitage, Fabergé eggs and carved ceremonial masks from Borneo. Stamps offered a path to everywhere, igniting the mind of a highly receptive young person. In addition, there was the satisfaction of owning things of value, things others might want. It was heady business. The world of man and nature and art and ideas was intimately confined in an album in my desk drawer. Today the internet might offer something of similar scope, but electronic instant flash transfer around the globe has none of the warmth and excitement of my personal journey with stamps.

In the following years I was distracted by studies and career demands. I narrowed my interest to stamps of the United States. This was more manageable. I became more interested in the delicacy of the engraving and variations in printing. I bought modestly, with some pretense of making a good investment, but really because I loved the stamps. With this maturing commercialized perspective, I went occasionally to a bourse or auction. These didn't fit my mood. It was panic like the opening bell on Wall street. When I was in graduate school my interest in stamps was reactivated. I lived in a rooming house with eight medical students. One of them was a stamp collector. He had been unusually opportunistic during the war. He was then in his early teens, and sat at home, avidly tracking the news. He sent letters to the postmaster of most of the cities that were identified, with an enclosed self-addressed envelope and a coupon purchased from the Universal Postal Union. This convention had been established by international agreement to assure delivery of a minimum weight letter anyplace among the participating nations. He had stacks of letters, addressed to himself, stamped and postmarked from every remote spot mentioned in the news. This exploded my dormant romance with stamps. He gave me a post-card from a young man with whom he had been corresponding who wanted to improve his English, and he said, "He will send you stamps."

I was a bit mature to be looking for a pen pal, but I decided to give it a try. This is how I came to meet Ivansevic Dragan. I didn't know which was his first and which was his last name. The only information I had beyond that was his address in Zadar, Jugoslavia. He was an enigma from the beginning.

I sent a brief note identifying myself as a replacement for Mr. Richard, as my predecessor was known to him. I indicated that he had become overwhelmed with his studies, and I would correspond to give him practice with English. Very promptly, almost by return mail, I received a postcard with a one line thank you to his new friend. It was typewritten, and signed, Ivansevic Dragan. I really couldn't determine if it ended with an '*r*' or an '*n*,' and I never resolved that in the months of our exchange. I thought he would get very little practice with English just typing postcards.

In a few weeks I received an envelope of Jugoslavia stamps. I began imagining what kind of person I had connected with. My old stamps from Bosnia and Herzegovina gave me a stereotype of robust men with full heads of hair and handlebar mustaches. My creative imagination assured me that he had been a freedom fighter during the war and had doubtless aided many Allied airmen shot down over the Balkans. I was uncertain how much to inquire because Jugoslavia was then a communist country, and all I knew was that it was a police state with Tito as dictator. This didn't appear very open or free and I didn't want to jeopardize my new friend's safety. I assumed I should pay for the stamps, but I had no idea of their worth. They were current stamps and not priced in the catalogues. I ventured to write and ask. I didn't know what the source was for them.

He replied he worked in the post office department. This immediately raised another delicate question in my mind, had he simply taken them out of the drawer, in other words stolen them. I couldn't hint at that, but I certainly didn't want this to be a temptation for him. My freedom fighter working in the postal service was a stretch for my imaginings, probably it was a position rewarding him for his wartime valor. I wanted to know if he needed food or clothing, so I asked. This shouldn't be too embarrassing, although as a privileged American I felt uncomfortable with it. Yes, he could use both. Again the question, how much? I bundled some clothes and canned goods and sent them off by the cheapest class possible.

Months later, I received a typed one line thank you. He didn't identify what he had gotten in the package. I didn't know if it had been split up, pilfered, or if he got the whole thing. I tried to inquire from the consulate in Chicago what was allowed, what could I send. Then came more stamps. This time there was a note saying these were scarce, and he had difficulty finding them. In my explorations I came across the name of a company that shipped bundles to Jugoslavia. I more or less remember the name, although I never knew for certain what it really was, considering the Cyrillic alphabet looks like backward *B*'s . I think it was Dobrovoljni Odbor. Anyway, I had an order blank and sent off some food and clothing as described. I assumed this was a sure thing.

Later, a note arrived, as vague as before. I knew he must be in a tight spot, under surveillance. Maybe his mail was censored. We had only a vague picture of what life was like there. The black and white postcards looked very uninspiring, and maybe there just wasn't anything worth writing about. More stamps kept coming. I was building up a big indebtedness, if I could ever figure out what and how much, and how to repay it.

On one card he said, "My mother asks how Mr. Robert is doing?" It sounded quaint, but made no sense. My freedom fighter, how old was he, and how old would his mother be? In frustration, I finally wrote and asked if we could exchange photographs. Certainly I wasn't learning anything about him from his one liners, and he wasn't getting much English practice.

His picture finally came. It was slightly larger than a postage stamp, the type of thing we used to get from a machine in the bus station for a quarter. This must have been a mistake. He was no bushy haired Serb with a handlebar mustache. He looked like a clerk, thin faced, straight hair, horn rimmed glasses and a narrow knotted necktie, that was crooked. After this he wrote more, occasionally by hand, in a small round script, really quite pretty, but not as I expected. He quoted mother often, just a few words that let me know she was still there.

He also made cryptic little comments along the margins, "My supply of food and clothes is getting bad." Immediately, I felt guilty. I sent him money, that probably ended up in the pocket of a censor. It was a most unsatisfactory exchange. How to break it off? How to equalize my debt, if there was one? I decided to tell him that I was getting married, and that I would have little time for correspondence. That ended it. Through the years, I wondered many time what had happened to him. Had he survived all the violence and savagery? I accused myself of abandoning him, and I was miserable with the memory. Shortly after this, I did get married and it occurred to me that at least I hadn't lied to him.

At the time of my wedding I received an unusual gift from my former student and roommate. It was for me, a stamped envelope or "cover." There was an accompanying note explaining what it was, how it came to be, and some indication of its worth. This was one of the self-addressed envelopes he had sent out to the war zones to be stamped and returned to him.

He had four covers, with different denomination stamps, that had been mailed from the Philippines, clearly postmarked: "Tacloban, Leyte." As his note explained, these had fortuitously arrived at the postmaster's desk just after MacArthur returned and liberated that part of the islands. To celebrate this, the local authorities had authorized an overprint of VICTORY. Of necessity, this was a crude handmade rubber stamp. After the Japanese invasion the stamps of the Philippines and the bullion had been hidden away in the jungle. Thousands were lost to humidity and the problems of storage, but by incredible chance, he had received four of his envelopes returned with these overprinted stamps. What made them additionally rare was that the rubber stamp had somehow been broken, or came loose, and it was reaffixed to the block with a pin. This was subsequently confirmed by the postal department. It produced a pinhead dot on one of the limbs of the V, and there it was in all its rarity, in my possession. I rushed to the library to confirm this in the Scott Catalogue.

Enough time had passed that there was a reference to this, but not in the detail the note had given. That was in a special study. There was no value given. It was blank, like the listing of a lobster on the menu. The catalogue listed many issues that were subsequently machine overprinted. There were millions of them, but only a few hundred of the broken hand stamped ones were known. The stamp I had was four centavos, showing a water buffalo. I was overwhelmed. I tried to return it to him, although it was a halfhearted effort. He insisted I keep it. I knew he was impulsive, and I expected he would regret it. He came to the wedding and reception. Then he graduated and we both moved on.

About ten years later, when I was pleasantly established, with a wife and two children, I was awakened at two o'clock in the morning by the phone. This wasn't all that unusual because I was a doctor, but the slurred heavy southern accent, jarred me. I didn't have many callers like that. Almost immediately, I knew who it was, even before he identified himself. I was certain he had been drinking.

"Old buddy, Ahm sittin' heah with a glass of Kentucky's smoothest, and Ah see a empty place on the wall where my Philippine covers are. One of them is missin', and you got it. Would you send it back?"

I was still fuzzy from sleep. I asked if he knew what time it was. He didn't answer. He was mostly repeating and mumbling to himself. "Yes sir, one's missin' and I got to have it back."

I said something like it was a wonderful gift and I cherished it, and it would always remind me of him, and it had been very generous.

He wasn't listening. "My momma's got half the silver bowls in the state of Florida. Some of this was buried when the Yankees came through, so you know its old. Ahl give you a bunch of that real wedding present stuff and you send back that envelope. Anything you want. Ya heah?"

I said, " I've got to get some sleep. Call me during the daytime and we can talk about it." I hung up and tried to sleep, but I couldn't.

Memories of things I hadn't attended to in the past flooded in. He was a strange young man, and with the passing years he doubtless had become more tangential. When we roomed together he frequently did spontaneous, dangerous and foolish things. They were dismissed as *youthful*. He drank more than the average, and one night in winter he brought to the house a burning marker lamp from a street construction site, and placed it in the basement. The next morning it was discovered because of the heavy smell and smoke from the burning oil. He couldn't remember having done it. A few weeks later he was throwing snow balls at the windows of Mt. Sinai hospital at midnight to attract the attention of the nurses. He was arrested and taken to jail. The university was notified and sent someone to offer legal assistance. In the morning he was in court, and with his vaudeville exaggerated southern accent he begged the forgiveness of the court, because "I never saw snow before, and I was overwhelmed." Of course, he was released. It was boyish exuberance.

At one of the class picnics he was plain out and out drunk. He was superman, and he tried to jump off a porch over its railing, but he didn't clear it and went crashing onto the driveway a few feet below, sliding along the gravel and cinders, severely scraping his hands and knees. He was unctuous and obsequious when the situation required. Those were just words until you saw him in action, arm around someone, leaning on him, overwhelming him. I got along with him because he was acutely aware of our difference in status, I was faculty and he was student. Certainly, his wedding gift was the result of an impulse he couldn't have explained, but he would have known at some level of awareness that it was a bribe. Just before giving up the idea of getting back to sleep, I recalled that I had heard he was arrested during his residency, for starting a fight with the hospital security force. The residency, incidentally, was in psychiatry. I was frightened. After this review of his earlier activities, in retrospect they were symptoms, I could only conclude he had become more erratic and impulsive. I knew he could come to get his letter, the next time he thought of it when he was drinking. I hadn't asked for his address, but I knew he would call again.

I decided on a devious plan. I would make a counterfeit cover and send it to him. He wouldn't know the difference. I am quite creative, and this was a challenge. I had some old envelopes that were slightly yellowed. They were standard business stock, the same as he had used. I had the common Philippine stamps, worth a few pennies. All that was needed was a handstamp of VICTORY and one for the cancellation that printed Tacloban. I went to an office supply store and ordered them. It was no problem. Next I photocopied the self

address he used from one of the lesser covers he had given me onto the old envelopes I had. This appeared as if it were typed by his own typewriter. I assembled these props and began work. I licked the water buffalo stamp and affixed it to the old, addressed envelope.

I then went to work on the rubber-stamps. I abused them. They had to be aged. I scrubbed them with a fine metal shoe brush we used on suede shoes. I scrubbed with scouring powder. I dipped them in acid. Finally, I hammered a small brad, with a rounded head like a pin, into the left limb of the V. I began to stamp on newspapers to get some idea of how much ink was needed. After I had inked the rubber-stamp, I stamped it three times on paper and then it had the proper, slightly worn, faint appearance. I did this with the VICTORY and the cancellation stamp. I made three envelopes, to see if I could improve my technique. They were essentially identical, almost perfect. As a last step, I placed them in a box with a small dish of hydrochloric acid and closed it. I checked often, and when they had yellowed very slightly, I was done. I inspected them every day to detect any flaw, and waited for the next call. The entire process had taken four days, mostly waiting for the rubber stamps.

Within a week he called again. I have no idea what reminded him or what determined that he should call. He called at a reasonable time, during the dinner hour, like a fund solicitor. He was sober and sounded congenial, certainly not menacing as he had before. He repeated his request to have the letter returned, and again he offered some treasures from his family's store of silver. I said I was very sorry that he wanted to take back the present because it had meant something special to me. I wanted to stir any sense of decent remorse he might have hidden deep in his being, so I added that I didn't want a substitute gift in return, because nothing could replace the thoughtful significance of the original.

For a brief moment I thought he faltered, and I had gotten through to him, but not so. I wouldn't have believed him anyway. It wouldn't last. I asked for his address, and said I would send it by registered mail at once. He became even more congenial and wanted to talk. I said I was going to eat, and hung up. It was the last time we talked. I put the envelope into a larger one, in preparation for mailing, and in doing this I inspected the three copies I had made, to select the best. I had first thought I would keep the real one and send a counterfeit, and wait for him to discover the switch. I doubted if he would have, because there was nothing to alert him to examine it in detail. It would simply have gone up on the wall with the others.

Then I paused, and thought I really don't want this. It would be too easy. I needed to disturb him. Why don't I send the original and one fake to him. I relished the consternation this would cause. He would have no idea how this came to be. He couldn't escape wondering which one was the original. He would have to send them off to an expert to be validated. I knew it would be enough of an irregularity to tarnish his pleasure in the real one and create some doubt about it, despite the expert's opinion. So I sent them. I never heard from him again. Later I tried to find him listed in the directory of the AMA and the various specialty boards, but he wasn't there.

₭ѓ

Through the years, I have waited quietly for one of the grandchildren to come to me with wide eyes and say, "Grandpa, will you show me your stamps?" It never happened. They were always too busy. Their lives are organized on a tight schedule. They don't appear to have hobbies, or collect anything. They have the internet and cell phones. They all have discovered soccer, and the boys have discovered girls, and the girls have learned the artifices that help the boys discover

them. So, I am left with a son-in law who collects stamps. That really is a satisfactory substitute, but my stamps have slipped from being an adventure to being a possession, so I will have to process the legal papers to transfer them to him at the appropriate time. Sadly, this isn't quite what I had hoped. It isn't the same as taking a little one by the hand and walking the yellow brick road together.

Chapter 37

Eternity

It was a travelogue closing scene. Without a ripple the sun slipped into the mirror of the western gulf, a pulsing crimson glow, framed by dappled clouds of corrugated gray purple, with peachblow light peeking through. Two minutes or slightly more, from the first indentation to the closing over the golden arc. It had swept the vault of sky in a smooth continuum, like a stoneless stream.

Had it repositioned, like a deliberate clock hand, after each spent moment, it would have fractured into countless shards, but with unhurried grace, the day gently sighed good night and went to sleep.

Fine sugar sand, the best beach in the world if you believed the Chamber of Commerce. That was easy to do because it seemed as perfect as we could imagine. The surf continuously rearranged the shore, rhythmic but irregular, large waves followed by a pause, and then often a small one, or with equal chance, a huge breaker that ran over your shoes even though you were a safe dry distance away. They played out their splash, and oozed back to the sea, scattering water bugs, small shells and foam bubbles along the retreating edge. And then it happened all over.

We walked here hand to hand before the doctor told us the results, only the lightest touch of finger tips, as if it would be easier to separate. It contrasted the bond of our hearts. The perpetual sea, the boundless freedom of the tides, the selfless motion of the universe,

minimized our anxious pain. We readied to become part of this with life winding down, but now the biopsy report was negative, and once more it was just a beach for swimming.

225

Chapter 38

Attitudes and Values

Big money, even just the appearances of wealth, overwhelms me. This view obviously represents a heightened disproportion between what I have, what I didn't have, and the indicators of what I interpret someone else has. Loose moving, lanky young men who wear Docker shoes without sox, and play tennis, always own a yacht. People of any age, especially women, who talk golf, belong to an exclusive country club. Middle aged men wearing starched shorts, and shirts with an alligator emblem on the pocket, buy their clothes from Abercrombie & Fitch. Platinum haired women, who stare from vapid gray eyes, are products of Eastern finishing schools, and probably live in the Hamptons. Blustering jocks usurp my living space, and challenge my right to drone on in my humble way. The out of bounds vitality of the young contrasts glaringly with my sedate lackluster. Irresponsible young drivers, with their quick and jerky confidence, threaten my measured reflexes. In this stereotypic world, I cringe behind my five degrees, searching for meaning in life. I am the metaphoric whimper.

My dichotomous black or white paradigm greatly reduces challenging options, but it is rigid and without flavor. I was led to this by the simplistic answers of my parents who attributed vexing problems to the consequences of original sin, but they were God-fearing, upstanding simple people so we should have received only a minimum dose of unworthiness. Later, in my more or less maturity, I tried to focus on a carry over from early life as we struggled to survive the great depression and even work in a few Freudian overtones. I don't know if my problem is genetic, contagious or just situational, but it is powerful and everpresent. I am in bondage, as driven as a salmon fighting upstream to spawn. Now with DNA testing available, I can probably identify extra alternatives, and blame a new combination of factors that gave me an inferior self-image. Hopefully, these will be more satisfying than *socio-economic forces beyond my control.* These are very difficult to work with, and don't provide much color or personal drama.

As I remember my earliest days, everyone seemed to be churning in the same pool, without many outstanding or exhilarating variables. It was murky and monotonous. Obviously, not everyone was imprinted in the same way I was, so there must be something else involved. The self-image is a delicate thing. It develops subliminally from so many unseen influences that are impossible to track, but there seem to be currents that persist, and in a sense are transmissible. My children might not agree, but I think they too have been tainted. I see in them occasional diffidence and a lack of confidence, or submissiveness, that I find so clearly in myself. As a well intentioned parent, I anguish over what I unwittingly may have done that bruised them.

Happily they do not even recognize this in themselves. They were launched from a higher social level than I, and have been bolstered so well they do not view any social dysfunction as being due to a deficiency. They are better compensated, and live in a state of relative assurance. All of my life I have conceded to those whom I judged to be better than myself, but I have resolved most firmly that this contagion must stop with me. I will not infect the next generation with my depressive, dour outlook. Just let them be blissful, naively content with their own resources. Thus far they have pleasantly surprised me and show little awareness of my nagging forebodings.

Chapter 39

Letter to Siblings

May 12, 2005

Dear Offsprings,

Mother and I have just returned home after a wonderful event. We want to share it with you. We were at the donor appreciation preview of the New Retzer Nature Center. This has just been completed. It is beautiful and wonderful, but you will have to see it for yourselves. All my words wouldn't be adequate. The building combines the Nature Learning Center with the Waukesha planetarium. It promises to become a major focal point among the county's educational facilities, and an inviting tourist attraction.

It is a thrilling miracle to those of us who had any involvement with getting it built. What inspiration enabled this to materialize when it seemed doomed after two rejected over-budget proposals. It represents an almost magical partnering between oftimes disparate factions, the private sector interests of tree huggers, bird watchers and the like, and the *official* governmental bureaucrats who are duty bound to educate our children and conserve our natural resources and beauty. Too often this is just lip service, and conflict.

While all of this was impressive, and a joy to observe and appreciate, our private joy was to share in Larry's quiet triumph. It was repeatedly acknowledged that, "Larry is a treasure," or other words to that effect. We really didn't need this, but if we had never fully appreciated him, it would have prompted us to take another look. This brings us to the real point in this communiqué.

Mother and I spent loving time reviewing our blessings: each of you. We certainly would have shared the specifics of the Retzer Nature Center with you, but that is only a small part of our story. As we looked around the room at the assemblage of civic leaders, educators, philanthropists and important people, we were overwhelmed to be included. Nothing in our modest accomplishments would merit that. You are our finest achievements, the quality of your lives and values, and if no one else had ever heard of you, we would still be overflowing with gratitude and pride. Look at yourself and your siblings, world class: naturalist, teacher of the year, artiste extraordinaire, and the least visible, probably the most compassionate geriatrician in the midwest. What family do you know of that has exceeded this roster. We thank you for giving meaning to our lives. As I have said to Mother repeatedly through the years, "If I didn't have you, I would want one just like you."

In awe at the wonder of it all,

US PUs, (Parental Units)

Chapter 40

Teacher of the Year

This is a response to an invitation to contribute to the notebook collection honoring the selection of Steve Kascht as Teacher of The Year. It was suggested we highlight his qualifications and performance as a teacher that resulted in this honor. We are not qualified to comment on these. However, we are qualified beyond all others, to describe Steve. He is our second born, but this is only in chronology. He is one of four equals, as the most wonderful member of our family. Please, don't expect an objective commentary.

Most simply, Steve is an excellent person. That says it all, and now we can begin rambling on to a few specifics, hopefully without revealing any embarrassing details. In his early childhood, he was simply cute and winsome. He was mischievous in grade school. When we received his report cards, we usually had very focused head to head confrontations. He tried to stare us down. I would counter his exophthalmic gaze with a stern parental demand that he desist trying to fake us out, and give some real explanations. All the while we tried not to look too sympathetic and loving.

There was one especially exciting exchange, when he was accused or trying to organize a book drop. He was in the sixth grade, I believe. Allegedly, he passed a note around the class directing everyone to knock a book to the floor at a precise time. This created the desired commotion. Poor Steve was accused. When we confronted him, he went into his charming misunderstood mode. I offered to defend him against the unfair nun, if he would just assure me that he was innocent.

I said, "Steve, I will take the note to the Chief of Police, who is a personal friend, and ask him to have the handwriting analyst compare a sample or your writing, and he will prove your innocence. If you say you didn't do it, I will believe it to my dying day."

It was touching, and it worked. He folded, and admitted he might have done it. We hugged him, and had no more problems; at least we didn't know of any.

One episode attests to his sweet generosity, and poor business sense. He had a paper route, and attended to his deliveries conscientiously, but he was casual about collecting. At times he graciously paid the bill with money from his allowance. One day he came home and announced that his class had collected enough money to buy a pagan baby. In those days it was common in parochial schools to salvage a Chinese infant from whatever horror and have it baptized. The class would then vote to select a name. Steve announced that it was a great honor that they chose the name Steve. It was some time before we learned that he had personally paid the entire twelve dollars from his own funds. What an example of Christian charity, not to mention buying popularity. He survived grade school.

In high school he was popular, elected to be student body president. He was also on the state champion mile relay team, and incidentally, he liked girls. He put in four years at Marquette as a pre-med, following our design for him. In the senior year he said he wanted to be a teacher. He enrolled for a fifth year to round out the requirements for an English major and get some education courses. As part of his independence and commitment, he became a dorm RA, worked in the parking ramp at 6:00am, then moved to the cafeteria and made orange juice. He was strongly motivated, and untiringly energetic.

GOOD GENES, LUCK, LOTS OF PRAYERS

We do not know directly if he has been a good teacher, but we do know he was a wonderful son: serious, sensitive, solicitous and fun. From this background he has grown into a most principled man, who would do well at anything he chose. It so happened he became a teacher; therefore, he must be a really good one. Q.E.D.

Chapter 41

Senior Retreat (1979)

Dear John,

We have been invited to write something for this special time, and even though we are a very verbal family, this is an opportunity to express to you things that might not otherwise be said.

We are immensely grateful for the blessings we have received, the greatest being the family. There is no way we can adequately catalogue the joys that you have brought to us, but think of all the good and wonderful things in your life, multiply that by four, and you have some measure of what it looks like from our view.

In the customary wisdom, parents are credited (or blamed) for having "raised" their children. This sounds so unilateral, much like growing radishes. Instead, it is a very interactive process. In the ideal, children help to change their parents. We have been extremely fortunate in this. Each of you has such special qualities and talents, special attitudes, personalities, interests and even special voices and mannerisms. You are wonderfully different, each from the other, and you express your love very individually.

You have required us to grow with you, and to respond to your special needs. For one or another of you we have argued with teachers and priests in defense of your integrity and rights, revised a school system, disrupted and expanded a parish budget,(we even bought extra football helmets) and developed a health room system.

In many, many ways we have had to be better and more involved than we would have been without you. For your sake, we have even tried to be interesting people.

As our last child, John, you have been fun and loving, but we realize through you that we are winding down. We are certainly not as vigorous and vital as we were with the others, although I don't let this show too much, and continue to pretend that I can still *lick* you. You have gently carried me along with my delusions.

We miss you these few days, knowing it is a foreshadow of the future. We are changing roles in many subtle ways, and in too short a time, you will be visiting us on Sunday afternoon, patting us patiently and wiping us off, but what a way to go. Johnnie, we love you very much.

The Grand Umbilicals,

Chapter 42

My Dearest Mary Beth

Dearest Mary Beth,

Congratulations on graduating from Medical School. You are the last of the family to complete the formal preparation for your life work. It seems appropriate that it should have taken such a long time. For the routine student this was mostly a matter of learning. For you it was also a tempering of your spirit. God has imposed some additional obstacles for you. With your physical problems, your suffering and limitations, you have increased your rapport on a common ground with those who will be your patients. Fortunately, it is not essential that a doctor have first hand experience with disease to be able to treat others effectively, but it is inevitable that this provides an extra dimension. It does give validity to the doctor, very much like Father Damien, who after years of service, finally addressed his parishioners as, "My dear fellow lepers."

Mother and I cherish especially the memory of you at the age of five, in your football helmet, unscrambling yourself, standing hands on hips and saying to your brothers, "Don't tackle so hard. I'm a lady, damn it." There have been very few instances (none as cute and cuddly) when you asked for special concession, but on the cosmic level, you have unknowingly had help. This may not be the easy path one would choose for comfort, but God has certainly given you the strength to endure your challenges, and the compassion to share other's problems. I predict warm and wonderful performance from you, and an endearing relationship with your patients.

I don't know if we will send this to you or not. Possibly, it might not have for you, the meaning intended. Probably some day this will surface in an unexpected context; maybe when we are writing our final instructions (along with detailed instructions for building the Hohokam canals).

We love you, daughter, and are tremendously proud of you.

Chapter 43

Fifty-Year Wedding Anniversary

September 22, 2001 – post 9/11/01

We have endured the gamut of EVIL. In recent days we have been emotionally shredded, and visually assaulted by scenes more surreal than the wildest connotation of that word. Ongoingly we have been inspired by noble rhetoric, which unfortunately ground on at times to fatigue and cliché.

We were left immersed in tragedy.

It is fortuitous that this gathering was planned when it was. We need it. A fifty-year anniversary is a traditional excuse for a celebration. Certainly, we were blessed to have been together so long, but mostly it was routine.

We simply put one foot in front of the other, day after day, and we survived.

Mary put up with me and earned abundant rewards in heaven. So, in our view, this celebration isn't about US. Our achievement isn't unique or really noteworthy. This is about YOU.

You have defined and bounded our world, and you have colored and flavored our lives with your individual diversity. From a pinpoint on the globe, designated Waukesha, you have created OUR entire universe.

GOOD GENES, LUCK, LOTS OF PRAYERS

In recent days, I heard among the inspiring words, a phrase attributed to FDR: "The warm courage of national unity." It is the same thing at a personal level. I would like to refocus this as it applies to the synergy of our lives. It is the steady presence of each of us offering interdependent support that builds an infrastructure able to withstand any adversity of body, soul or politics. We thank you deeper than words for being that part of our lives.

Chapter 44

The Golden Patina

Doing anything for fifty years should qualify one as an expert. Not so with marriage. It testifies to endurance, but it doesn't assure expertise. There may not be many surprises, but each new day presents the potential for challenge. Patience and tolerance develop in abundance and are tested unendingly. Monotony hums in the background. Disaster lurks behind every pending moment, just one misstep away. All of this is lumped together under the file heading of Love. Memories are the greatest bonus from all this living. They are there, ready for recall, but are not guaranteed or automatic. They require some tending, maybe even polishing and embellishing. Living is chronologic. Reliving is sporadic and often capricious. It is looking into a kaleidoscope upside down, and depends on the vagary of association.

Deep, deep inside of me
Where even my mind can't peek,
Are feelings of hidden silence,
That surely must be asleep.
I cannot arouse them
By a focused beam of thought,
But rather they must float
Freely without being sought.

GOOD GENES, LUCK, LOTS OF PRAYERS

Mary and I met as the result of the well-intentioned meddling of a nursing school classmate, who was recently married to a fellow resident at St. Mary's hospital. She was still in a post-nuptial pink haze, and thought all the world should be similarly blest. We were invited to a blind date dinner. Mutually, we were unwillingly surprised, the tender beauty and the ever so eligible young doctor. In simple truth, she was the yummiest variation on the standard blueprint I had ever gotten close to. Predestination was evident in the rapid tempo of the courtship. We met May 6th and married September 22th. This was most uncharacteristic for me, but probably more consistent with the working of the female game plan. We have never resolved the issue of who proposed to whom, but I admitted to myself that I was ready to surrender on our first encounter. I feigned aloofness for a few days because I knew flaws would surface. Certainly she had some obscure hideous defect, otherwise why would she still be floating on the open market?

She was two years out of nurses training, and was working for a doctor downtown. From her accounts, and the evidence of my acute clinical eye, I knew she was breezy and trivial, flitting around on high heels, squandering money on clothes and cosmetics, and dangling hapless young men, but I thought I saw something more. She was energetic and fun, and very affectionate, so I forgave her. In our negotiations and disclosures, we discovered that despite deceptive appearances, we were really quite insecure, and that we needed each other, so we decided to gamble and go for it. We survived, and five months stretched into fifty years plus. We assumed different roles. Mary was intelligent and quick, but she wasted little time trying to appear profound. She was enthusiastic and usually optimistic. As a good nurse she was pragmatic and did whatever had to be done without making a big production. To her life was for living. She left the ruminating and worrying to me. I did it excessively well, and thus we maintained a steady balance.

In the first year of marriage we were happy. Mostly we were exploring and discovering what each other was all about. Our four months of so-called courtship certainly didn't provide enough common ground to justify a decision to marry. We had scarcely defined superficial likes and dislikes. I learned that Mary liked lamb and herring. I reacted strongly against each of them. This was about the level of our rapport in the first year. Fortunately, these differences were of little consequence. We didn't have any serious conflicts. We did the requisite newly married things. We showed off our wedding presents, talked about ambiguous plans, went about smiling and gave overblown indication that ours was the best of all possible worlds. We proudly displayed each other.

I suspect that we were most relieved to realize that we probably had not made a mistake.

Certainly, most couples think they are happy in the first year, but they don't know what they have gotten into. *Happy* is about all they expect, and it isn't an in depth judgment. It requires longer than that to discover enough differences to come to any other conclusion. In this context, *happy* is an empty word. It has no firm basis. It means whatever is expected, more a matter of convention than conviction. It is post-nuptial meringue, and like any excess, it becomes cloying, and the stage is set for a revision, if not open revolution.

Our marriage did not evolve beyond this first honeyed stage, because I was called into the Air Force and sent to France. The mutual development of our marriage molecule was temporarily on hold. However, it was exactly this interruption that gave me my first awareness of how much I needed Mary. Being married was the first time in my life I had a sense of completeness, a plateau, instead of constant shifting from one temporary status to another. I had arrived at something that seemed stable and was enjoyable. Then, with this abruptly taken away, I began to crumble.

Now I came to my first appreciation of Mary as an element in my life beyond being pretty and pleasant. She received a terse telegram to the effect that I had been relieved of duty, transferred to patient status and flown to the hospital in Wiesbaden. The Red Cross offered a few meaningless comments, but nothing could explain adequately. Mary applied for dependent travel orders, packed a few things, took little Larry by the hand and spent two weeks on a troop transport. She arrived in Germany, and we began a deeper phase of our marriage. I was assigned to duty as a pathologist in the headquarters hospital. With Mary's contribution, we were easily assimilated into its family circle, and it was soon forgotten that I had been a problem. Without her I could have been discarded.

This was quite a performance for a young lady who had never been outside of Wisconsin. The time in Europe was wonderful. We regarded it as a second honeymoon. When we returned to civilian life, the real, long term phase of our marriage began. I joined the faculty of the newly opened University of Miami Medical college. Life looked very promising, but new uncertainties began gnawing at me. I returned to the security of an extended residency, and began psychiatric therapy to rid myself of the gray shadows of Chateauroux. Again, Mary was in full bloom at the masthead of our public image, and a steady marshmallow for the family. I stabilized, and mostly satisfied my expectations. We had a supportive religious climate in the family, and without too much theology, it has been most gratifying throughout our lives. I would like to retrace highlights of our journey together. A random selection of events and anecdotes should portray the many flavors of her personality better than a thesaurus of adjectives. It is the lodestar advice given to young writers: *show don't tell,* so we sample a potpourri.

GOOD GENES, LUCK, LOTS OF PRAYERS

ℰᏋ

As we began in Waukesha, planning for a lifetime, Mary entered into the usual things. She used her nursing skills at St. Mary's grade school health room and also became expert with jammed zippers. She was in the mothers' group and carpool of the newly formed Montessori school. She joined the Waukesha Service Club, mastered the cash register, and acquired the wisdom and skills of marketing, eventually becoming the chair of the Thrift and the Hospital Gift shops. She remembers proudly that she organized a manual that for a few years was the unofficial Bible.

She had come from a background of Big Band music and was a good dancer. I had never been to a dance, other than a forced pairing with my girl cousin at the YW. Inevitably we took dancing lessons, and got involved with a group of like minded hopefuls. Mary hadn't spent much time in the kitchen. Although her mother and grandmother were good cooks, she needed a bit of fine tuning, so she took a variety of classes. The most memorable was from Richard Graussman, who bestowed a small certificate proclaiming her to be a graduate of the Cordon Bleu. We took some classes together. One was from Dennis Getto, who was the food and restaurant critic for the Milwaukee Journal. To avoid recognition, so he could do his evaluations unknown, he came to class wearing dark glasses, a pig nose and a porkpie hat.

Mary developed an interest in painting. She enrolled in classes of oil painting with a succession of quite ordinary teachers, but she produced some enjoyable, quality works.

Then she switched to watercolor, and never felt as confident with that medium. She accompanied me three times to the University of Iowa Summer Writing Festival, and enrolled once in a class, certain that her past was worth recording. She wrote an account of a food fight in the disturbed ward during nursing training, but after that she left the literary aspirations to me. During these middle years, she was an enjoyable companion, and a steady associate in our efforts to raise four kids.

She occasionally did spontaneous, quirky, one of a kind things, that are fun in recall. They must indicate some pixy genes. When we had our farm, I bought a '49 Ford pickup truck. I had it loaded with fence, a brush cutter and other tools and was going to take it to the farm. Mary was to follow me in the station wagon with the kids. I was rolling along I-57 on our usual route, and passed the state patrol weigh station without a second thought. A minute later I was overwhelmed by flashing lights and a siren. The trooper motioned me to pull over, then started walking toward me. At that strategic moment Mary pulled along side, rolled down the window and shouted, "well, what did you do this time?" It implied that I was an habitual criminal. Even the officer chuckled, as I explained that I really didn't know I was a truck, subject to the weight regulations, and No, I wouldn't do it again. I just followed him back to the scales and proved I was under 40,000 pounds. Mary didn't feel any responsibility at all.

On one occasion we were flying to a meeting and had to change planes in Minneapolis. Our flight from Milwaukee was delayed because of fog, so we arrived a half hour late. As we chugged and puffed up to the gate, the attendant said, "I'm sorry, but I just gave your seats to someone else."

I started a loud explosion, complaining she knew we were coming, they had called ahead to hold the plane a few minutes. "Oh, don't worry, we aren't overbooked, you just won't be sitting together."

I yelled that I wanted to sit with my wife. Then Mary said, from some place in outer space, "Now dear, don't get excited. You know you might have another heart attack." Suddenly we had seats together.

GOOD GENES, LUCK, LOTS OF PRAYERS

In something of the same vein of the unexpected, in the evening of the day she had back surgery for spinal stenosis, the patient sharing the other half of the curtain divided room had noisy visitors. Mary, somewhat woozy from medication, got out of bed, pulled open the folding divider and said, "I have just had major surgery today. Would you mind being more quiet?"

It's an old fashioned word, but I think *spunky* is appropriate. I have repeatedly been impressed that when Mary had real pain, post surgical, or chemotherapy, she had the pain threshold of a gladiator, but day to day things like dry skin or dandruff could set her off into a litany of anguish and complaints.

I cherish a cute image of her, hunkered down in a corner of the book department of Harrod's, furtively copying recipes for scones. She even ate haggis so she might have better rapport with our romantic son who sought, and was adopted by the Maclaren clan. I got by without much sacrifice, only sampling single malt whisky.

Mary was ever eager to be everything she thought I wanted. When we traveled as a family, the pool at the motel was often more crucial to the kids than the awesome scenery. I shared their pleasure, but Mary was not happy in the water. She sat and read poolside. One birthday she presented to me a little certificate that proclaimed the successful completion of a *fear of water* course. Sometime later I led her, tense and halting, into the shallow end. She could never float face down without the reassuring slightest touch of my finger. Wishful effort has limitations.

The idyllic life we had in the dream home we built in country, turned into a haunting memory after we experienced a window break in the middle of the night. It was apparently a senseless and random act, probably a prank. Mary relived the spray of shards across her bed, night after night, and couldn't sleep. She went to St. Paul and stayed with Mary Beth. They visited an indoor shooting range, perhaps intending to take a lesson in the use of a handgun. Instead, Mary bought a little canister of pepper spray and came home, somewhat fortified. I slept with a twenty gauge shotgun between us in bed. It wasn't enough. We moved. She occasionally has a flashback, and is remorseful about the change in our dream plans this forced on us.

‟⁜

On occasions I feel a twitch from an intuitive center in my brain, deep to hearing and voice, that challenges me, "Didn't you expect it would be like this. Weren't you paying attention?"

Of course I was listening. I had to say, "I do," at the right time. After all it was my wedding too. I had lots of things on my mind, more than just how many bridesmaids there were. I had never done this before. I know she had been thinking about it since grade school, but it was quite a surprise for me that I was actually there. I certainly wasn't focused on the fine print, all that stuff about for richer or poorer and for better or for worse. I knew it would go the way we planned. With all the excitement and energy and the whole future ahead of us, who would take that part seriously? Well that's not quite true. I really meant it when I said, "Yes." I just didn't think the *for worse* meant me, or us, and I knew it couldn't happen. Now, fifty years down the line, this is the part that means the most. In the dark of early morn, as I look to the new day, I think of what could I do to make her life easier and more meaningful. I feel how draining it is, how much energy is wasted just doing simple things that once were spontaneous, and how frustrating to listen to my demanding, hearty cheerleading. I kiss her sleeping cheek, and know I can't really change things. This is my life's most tender time, when I know she suffers, not just pain, but the awareness she is winding down, and I can't help. I only pray I can stay with her.

Chapter 45

Heaven Won't Wait

The future insistently pushes into my peripheral view, ever more impatient, forcing an awareness of the great imbalance between the time past and the days yet uncounted. No pretense or deception can soften this. It is sobering, but I have few regrets, and happily, no festering unfulfilled goals. Aging is inexorable, but it is not a uniform process. For some it is a graceful, almost imperceptible, decline. In others it is a jerky succession of dysfunctions. Some resist, in blustering denial, and contend that age confers the privilege of erratic or whimsical behavior that would be unacceptable in an earlier stage of life. I certainly do not plan to change the measured tempo of my ways with unnatural out of bounds excesses. I am not frantic to get in my last lick, or waggle my ears and stick out my tongue in defiance. Neither do I hold with the embittered prescription to "Rage at the dying of the light." This is a put-on, setting us against the immutable fact, between the eternal rock and a cosmic hard place.

In Eastern cultures there is acceptance of the changing capacity of the aged, and an ongoing revision of their appropriate role. In the fourth ashrama, the proper posture is resignation, when one rejects material things, yields control and readies for the long journey, "from whose bourn no traveler returns."

I relish an idealized image of my grandfatherly role, sitting before a quiet fire, in patched-elbow cardigan, leather bound volume in hand, reading to the children spread on the floor around me. I probably will actually settle for something less overdone than this Norman Rockwell scene. I yearn for time to reflect, and for a gourmet retaste of the nuances of my life. I will invite select friends to share flashback vignettes, reliving former successes and glories, as we justify our existences with a recasting of *"It's a Wonderful Life."* I hope to remain thus composed and unthreatened, and able to make the great transition without tripping at the exit.

I feel vaguely superstitious that writing these thoughts might precipitate an unwanted premature event. I know a writer who confessed that she no longer says her childhood prayer: "Now I lay me down to sleep..." because she didn't want to direct the Lord's attention to herself. Certainly, I do not want to riffle the pages of time at an accelerated pace. All of this introspection has given Mary and me increased awareness of each other's feelings and needs. During dark times in the past, we have talked with God, renewed our commitment to each other, and found calm. It should be the same in this coming challenge. We will spend good times weaving in and out of memories that are as vivid as today, until there are no more todays.

഻ഓ

> From cover to cover,
> It's a lonely journey
> From the beginning
> Until it's over.

Chapter 46

Stewardship

When I no longer am
How will the world survive?
The sun may rise
But will it charm the day
Without my welcoming eyes?
Will flowers still smile
And breathe their sweetness
Without my reassurance?

My gentle spouse distraught
After so many tender years,
And the earth, my primal love
Since first energy we shared,
Will feel my ardor lost.

Can the world withstand
And still be as it was,
Or is it slowly winding down
Decreased by each one gone?
Even the earthbound God
With all the troubles of creation,
May miss a chatty confidant.

The earth and I
Have mutually enriched,
But now it all has passed
Without a pause or flicker
On the cosmic seismograph.

Chapter 47

Secrets

What spaces the teeth
In the combing wind
As it curries the sugar sand?

Lines loose and gentle
Like tossed hair
Of a young girl running,

Or parallel tight
Engraved and sure,
Fingerprints of the unknown.

Who keys the pitch
Or sets the tone,
From scented murmur
To keening gale?

You will know,
But only when
It's too late to tell.

Chapter 48

Requiem

As we review the high times of our lives, those moments of overpowering beauty and meaning, against the oncoming shadow of inevitable surrender and resignation, we are prayerfully grateful for the vibrance of living them. We cannot hold forever what we once were privileged to use, but our memories survive as pale reminders of the intensity with which we lived wonders others may have never known.

About the Author

Bob Kascht is a retired physician who lives in Waukesha,Wisconsin with his wife, Mary Ann. For thirty years as a pathologist he studied and described diseases and tumors, and honed his powers of observation. In the last twenty years he changed his focus, refined his vocabulary and expanded his interests to include documentation of human foibles and musings about the meaning of it all. He has a wide range of interests, especially the world of nature, the outdoors and concerns for ecology. His offspring provide a stimulating diversity: a naturalist, a literature teacher, a physician and an artist. Family gatherings are very spirited. He is an ardent admirer of Lewis Thomas who also is a physician, a pathologist and a writer, and Aldo Leopold, who needs no listing of credentials. He is more than slightly devoted to Thoreau and Robert Frost.

ഹ൫

Photos of the Kascht and Rubert Families

ഹ൫

Bob Kascht - Camelot Regained

Mary Kascht

Grandma Rubert

Grandpa Frank

Grandpa Frank Rubert - The Butcher

Grandma Esther

Kascht - The German Helix

The Rubert Family
Left to Right: Carrie, Eunice, Max's father, Frank, Esther,
Lawrence, Delight, Max (front)

The Kascht Family

The Long Shadow

Printed in the United States
126086LV00002B/47/P